CRACKING THE WIRE

DURING BLACK LIVES MATTER

CRACKING THE WIRE
DURING BLACK LIVES MATTER

Edited by

Ronda Racha Penrice

Cracking The Wire During Black Lives Matter
©2022 Ronda Racha Penrice
All Rights Reserved.

Cover by Art Sims
Edited by David Bushman
Book design by Scott Ryan
Interior photos courtesy of HBO

Published in the USA by Fayetteville Mafia Press
Columbus, Ohio

Contact Information
Email: fayettevillemafiapress@gmail.com
Website: fayettevillemafiapress.com
Instagram: @fayettevillemafiapress
Twitter:@Fmpbooks

ISBN: 9781949024289
eBook ISBN: 9781949024296

Dedicated to Michael K. Williams
"Omar's Coming"

CONTENTS

Part 3: All Systems Down

Part 4: The Incredible Lightness of Being Omar and Michael K. Williams

INTRODUCTION

Cracking *The Wire* During Black Lives Matter

By Ronda Racha Penrice

Pick a show or film you like, and chances are someone from *The Wire* is in it. Idris Elba, Jamie Hector, Wood Harris, Michael K. Williams, Wendell Pierce, Sonja Sohn, Seth Gilliam, Clarke Peters, Michael B. Jordan, Lance Reddick, Chad L. Coleman, Hassan Johnson, also known as Stringer Bell, Marlo Stanfield, Avon Barksdale, Omar Little, Bunk Moreland, Kima Greggs, Ellis Carver, Lester Freamon, Wallace, Cedric Daniels, Dennis "Cutty" Wise, Roland "Wee-Bey" Brice, and more have appeared in such films and TV shows as *The Suicide Squad*, *Bosch*, *Empire*, *Lovecraft Country*, *Suits*, *The Chi*, *The Walking Dead*, *Da 5 Bloods*, *Creed*, *John Wick*, *All American*, and *For Life*. For Black actors, *The Wire* was a game-changer.

Yes, television has had outstanding Black talent in dramatic roles. *St. Elsewhere* had Denzel Washington and Alfre Woodard, Blair Underwood was on *L.A. Law*, and Andre Braugher was on *Homicide: Life on the Street*. Their roles, however, were professional ones as doctors, a lawyer, and a detective. When it came to television, Black characters who were working-class or below the poverty line were largely rendered invisible. So *The Wire* was unique in that it gave a voice to the many Black people the larger society threw away while also showcasing professionals like Baltimore Mayor Clarence Royce, played by Glynn Turman, whose 1975 film *Cooley High* remains a classic; Frankie Faison's Ervin H.

Burrell, acting commissioner to Mayor Royce; and several high-ranking Baltimore Police rank and file, including Robert Wisdom's police Major Howard "Bunny" Colvin and Lance Reddick's Cedric Daniels, who eventually rises to police commissioner. By today's standards, with such shows as the John Singleton-created *Snowfall* and *Raising Kanan* and *BMF*, produced by rapper and former drug dealer 50 Cent, *The Wire* might not seem as groundbreaking to some. But in 2002, television did not have multidimensional Black characters representing this underclass, and certainly not in such abundance as on *The Wire*. For a lot of television viewers, *The Wire* was the first drama series with Black characters to significantly dig beyond the "thug number one, two, or three" invisibility status to which many of the numerous cop shows relegated them. This was a huge breakthrough back in 2002.

In *The Wire*, heroin is the drug, but crack is the ethos, or the relatable point of entry to the time in which it aired. Crack, a cheap form of the powder cocaine pop culture promoted as glamorous, flooded urban communities, overwhelming and devastating them. As more young Black men began to sell crack in hopes of gaining the prosperity the menial jobs largely awaiting them could not offer, the increased competition, especially as guns became more plentiful, resulted in violence and a high death toll. Between 1984 and 1994, homicide rates for Black males ages fourteen to seventeen more than doubled, according to "Measuring Crack Cocaine and Its Impact" by Roland G. Fryer Jr., Paul S. Heaton, Steven D. Levitt, and Kevin M. Murphy, scholars affiliated with Harvard University and the University of Chicago, published in 2006. Homicides of Black males ages eighteen to twenty-four almost matched that rate. During this same period, rates of Black children in foster care more than doubled, while fetal death rates and weapons arrests for Black people rose more than 25 percent. Although crack was highly addictive, government and media response to those who fell prey was a far cry from that of the later opioid crisis, which was deemed as impacting largely White Americans. So while Black crack addicts were locked up, White opioid addicts would be sent to treatment. As crack was portrayed as *only* an urban problem, a Black problem, the media hid the many White crack addicts. This perception of crack as a Black nuisance was used to justify the continued overpolicing of Black communities.

Disparities in sentencing for crack cocaine and powder cocaine became huge. "In 1986, before the enactment of federal mandatory minimum sentencing for crack cocaine offenses, the average federal drug sentence for African Americans was 11 [percent] higher than for whites. Four years later, the average federal drug sentence for African Americans was 49 [percent] higher," according to the American Civil Liberties Union's 2006 report "Cracks in the System: 20 Years of the Unjust Federal Crack Cocaine Law." To give further context, possession of five grams of crack cocaine resulted in an automatic minimum sentence of five years, while it took five hundred grams of powder cocaine to match that, even though powder cocaine is essential to producing crack and is the far more powerful drug between the two.

Two years before *The Wire*, HBO aired the six-part miniseries *The Corner*, based on the 1997 nonfiction book *The Corner: A Year in the Life of an Inner-City Neighborhood* by David Simon and Ed Burns, one a *Baltimore Sun* reporter and the other a former Baltimore policeman turned Baltimore public school teacher, both White, exploring a Black family wracked by drug addiction as they struggle to survive in a West

Producer Nina Noble and *The Wire* creator David Simon on the set of *The Corner* in 1999. Photo courtesy of David Simon's Twitter account

Baltimore community with an active drug market. That miniseries was directed by Baltimore native Charles Dutton, beloved by Black audiences for his Baltimore-set comedy series *Roc* (with a dramatic flair), which ran from 1991 to 1994, and adapted by Simon and David Mills (now deceased), Simon's college friend and fellow journalist, who was Black. It is the foundation of *The Wire*, with the TV series *Homicide: Life on the Street*, sparked by Simon's 1991 nonfiction book *Homicide: A Year on the Killing Streets*, chronicling the Baltimore Police Department Homicide Unit, also playing a role. When *The Wire* premiered on June 2, 2002, it was the first series dedicated to exploring the complex web presented by this drug era.

As Black audiences tuned in, many scrambling to find HBO and add it, and others catching it at other people's houses or on bootleg video, White viewership, and praise, was limited. So much so that, as *The Guardian's* Shane Danielsen noted in "*The Wire*: Too Black, Too Strong," on the heels of another Emmy shutout for the series, "in its six seasons, *The Wire* has never once been in the running for the major prize," meaning best drama. That was just over four months after the series ended, on March 9, 2008. "The show is simply too urban. And by 'urban,' of course, I mean 'black,'" he wrote. "Black TV shows, like black films, are meant solely for black audiences, so the thinking goes—and, as such, are rarely permitted to penetrate the cultural mainstream."

As aforementioned, the love bestowed on *The Wire's* many Black actors, who, Danielsen wrote, accounted for over 70 percent of the cast, is evident because of the other series and movies they keep showing up in. That love definitely cannot be found in the so-called holy grail of award shows or industry recognition. As impossible as it is to believe today, none of the actors from *The Wire* received Emmy nominations. Not one! Thank goodness for the NAACP Image Awards, which recognized Idris Elba's Stringer, Sonja Sohn's Kima, Michael K. Williams's Omar, Wendell Pierce's Bunk, and Glynn Turman's Mayor Royce. Sohn, Williams, and Pierce even received multiple nominations. With other shows, it's regularly acknowledged that the actors breathe life into the characters. Unfortunately, Black actors are too rarely given credit for their craft, especially when the setting is an urban one. Instead, the presumption is they are not acting, that they are just playing themselves. During *The Wire*'s era, that presumption definitely seemed to be the case with Black actors aside from a chosen handful, as they rarely received acknowledgment for their craft by the recognized entities. *The Wire*'s extraordinary performances suggest a heartfelt desire, and responsibility even, to get it right. This was no thug-number-one or thug-number-two situation. These people were not disposable, largely because the actors playing them wouldn't let them be. To them, they mattered, and that's what came through the TV screen.

Speaking on Clubhouse about their experiences on *The Wire* in January 2021, Julito McCollum, Tristan "Mack" Wilds, Maestro Harrell, and Jermaine Crawford, who played Namond Brice, Michael Lee, Randy Wagstaff, and Duquan "Dukie" Weems respectively, spoke of how Baltimore embraced them, with residents even inviting them to dinner. Jamie Hector, who was attending the Savannah College of Art and Design (SCAD) aTVfest in 2019 in support of his character Jerry Edgar on the Amazon Prime Video series *Bosch*, shared with me how Baltimore cats took him aside and schooled him on how they walked and moved, as opposed to how New Yorkers did it, for Marlo Stanfield, because it was just that important to them for him to get it right. "We always knew we were doing something special for us," Hector shared on *The Bakari Sellers Podcast* during a June 2021 appearance, after Sellers basically asked if he and his fellow *Wire* actors knew how impactful the show would be.

We grew to love, hate, or at least understand these people society so often hid because of Hector and *The Wire*'s other talented cast members. They brought dignity to those who looked like them. In some cases, their own personal experiences gave them the compassion they needed for their characters to be authentic. For Omar, played by Brooklyn native Williams, and Snoop, portrayed by Baltimore's own Felicia Pearson, who got to keep her real nickname, this rang true. There was a truth to their characters fed by their journeys on the rough side of the streets. Williams got his signature scar from being slashed by a razor during a bar fight. Pearson was truly *The Wire*, running her own corners and even serving prison time for murder. As the saying goes, "Game recognizes game," as the saying goes, and Williams, as is well-known, saw Pearson in a Baltimore bar and invited her to set. He knew she was the real deal, and the rest of us learned that too. While the actors on *The Wire* almost strictly adhered to the words written on the page, Pearson, revealed Burns in Jonathan Abrams's essential 2018 book, *All the Pieces Matter: The Inside Story of The Wire*, was permitted to improvise her dialogue.

This doesn't mean there was no acting involved. Quite the contrary. Those who assumed Williams especially essentially played himself as Omar were greatly mistaken. He has disproved that in many subsequent performances, including his role as bootlegger Chalky White in HBO's triumphant period piece *Boardwalk Empire*, where he held his own against the great Jeffrey Wright, who played Harlem crime boss Valentin Narcisse. And when he shockingly passed away in September 2021, his genius as an actor, along with his compassion as a human being, was widely acknowledged. His subsequent roles included Jack Gee in the HBO movie *Bessie*, about the legendary blues singer Bessie Smith, which scored him his about-damn-time first of five Emmy nominations; former boxer/criminal Freddy in *The Night Of*; gay activist Ken Jones in the miniseries *When We Rise*; the powerless father Bobby McCray in Ava DuVernay's emotional Netflix limited series *When They See Us*, about the Exonerated Five, formerly known as the Central Park Five; and closeted father Montrose Freeman in the Jim Crow-set series *Lovecraft Country* on HBO, for which he received what would be his final Emmy nomination.

During an on-set interview for the 2018 remake of *Superfly* I did with him in Atlanta for theGrio, he shared how he had changed the script and flipped typecasting on its head. "When I started seeing that there was a pattern, I guess for lack of a better word, in the types of roles that I was being cast for, I was like 'You know what, Mike, this is my vehicle, the urban character, and I know urban pretty damn well,' and I decided to wear it as a badge of honor. And with that, I decided to bring some respect, dignity, empathy, and compassion to these characters that people, that society, sees as menaces." Clearly, his other *Wire* castmates had the same agenda.

Given David Simon's background as a crime reporter, many of *The*

Wire characters were an extension of those he encountered in his earlier work. Andre Royo's Bubbles, for instance, is inspired by a man known as Possum, who played the same role in real life. Many *Wire* fans know that Baltimore's own 1970s-1980s-era heroin kingpin Melvin Williams, who even played a deacon on the show, is the blueprint for Avon Barksdale. The *New York Times* even led with that factoid in this headline for his December 2015 obituary: "Melvin Williams, an Inspiration for 'The Wire,' Dies at 73." Stringer Bell is said to be inspired by a trio of Baltimore drug dealers—Stringer Reed, Roland Bell, and Kenneth A. Jackson. Meanwhile, Dennis "Cutty" Wise is reportedly based on a contract killer connected to Vernon Collins, another Baltimore heroin dealer and the inspiration behind Wee-Bey Brice. Oscar "Rick" Requer is the real-life sketch for Bunk. And the list goes on and on.

Some of this explains why *The Wire* still feels so real to so many people, especially those unfamiliar with the conditions of the characters here. One of *The Wire*'s most enduring legacies is its recognition that people in urban areas, the ghetto to some, the hood to others, are people too to those who have been taught to believe otherwise. People like me, who came of age in an area on the South Side of Chicago nicknamed the "Wild 100s," didn't need *The Wire* to know that police regularly beat up Black people or that justice was hard to come by for us or even that public schools were not set up or equipped to educate us. But it's always nice to be acknowledged. And with television, it's been a long time coming. But with *The Wire*, other people saw it too.

Unlike in other shows in which Black people came and went, we were, save for *The Wire*'s second season, a very dominant presence on the show. Viewers got to know these characters, so if they were killed, it mattered. That loss hurt. With *The Wire*, it wasn't just our problems on display, but also our humanity. That's what our first three writers—Odell Hall, Sheree Renée Thomas, and Ed Adams—share in Part 1 of this book, "Pieces of the Familiar." That sense of connection and knowing. That feeling of being seen and recognized.

Still, *The Wire* revealed some of the very challenges poor or struggling Black folks faced that were not uttered out loud back then when the show started. These are some of the issues—be it the school system, diversity and equity in the mainstream media, institutional failure of Black people, or *The Wire*'s Black woman problem—that Mekeisha Madden Toby, Danian Darrell Jerry, Seve Chambers, Adom M. Cooper, and I myself explore in Part 3, "All Systems Down."

Historically speaking, this country has long been rigged against us. Contrary to some people's claims, slavery was not a choice. And while Maryland might not appear so Southern in the twenty-first century, it was very much a slaveholding state during the antebellum era. It was a place where slavery thrived well into the Civil War. When Abraham Lincoln issued the Emancipation Proclamation on January 1, 1863, he exempted Maryland because it was a border slave state that sided with the Union. *The Wire* never fully explored those details, but the weight of that history reveals itself in almost everything, and in *The Wire*, it was present to those who didn't even know how to recognize it. According to *Racial Wealth Divide* in Baltimore, a 2017 report from the Racial Wealth Divide Initiative at the Corporation for Enterprise Development, the average White household in Baltimore possessed two times the wealth of the average Black household. That disparity, despite what some would have you believe, has nothing to do with lack of desire and hustle. Money plays a central role in *The Wire*, with a lot of the decisions that are made being motivated by the promise of getting it.

Leaving out these details hasn't diminished *The Wire*'s value. To a lot of Black people, *The Wire* is still the greatest TV show ever. Some of the things folks criticize the show for not being explicit about are things that, for others, always lurk in the background. So imagine my surprise when a very popular Black director I cannot name informed me that he had never watched it. He said he'd tried, but just couldn't get over the show's White gaze. By contrast, a film publicist I know who works with some of the best directors and producers in the industry informed me that she *literally* watches *The Wire* every single day and has basically done so since the show first aired in 2002. In fact, it is how she and her now husband first bonded. For her, *The Wire* is packed with so many life lessons that help her navigate the pressures of the world even today.

But the director's comments still got me thinking. It was not that he was too young to watch *The Wire*. He was actually in his teens when the show came out. Is it crazy to think *The Wire* has a White gaze when its main creative driver, David Simon, generally grew up in predominantly White environments and came across inspirations for a lot of the characters covering the crime beat for the White-owned *Baltimore Sun*? On top of that, the DC-born Simon, who was raised in Montgomery County, Maryland, attended Bethesda-Chevy Chase High School, a public school that is still considered among the best academically and to this day remains predominantly White—just not so overwhelmingly so, with its diverse population measuring in at over 40 percent. When Simon was a student back in the 1970s, working on the student newspaper, B-CC, as it is known, was still in the process of "welcoming" in Black students. Unlike other predominantly White schools in the United States, which were largely White on purpose, B-CC first got Black students in the 1960s.

In the 1970s, Montgomery County, according to its own planning department, was nearly 95 percent White. Flip through the University of Maryland, College Park, yearbook from 1983, the year Simon graduated, and you will see that it too is predominantly White. As was the *Baltimore Sun*, where he was a reporter for over a decade. Norman T. Wilson, who rose to night editor at the *Sun*, was among the first Black reporters hired there, in the 1970s, but the staff was (and still is) predominantly white, as in most newsrooms of established mainstream papers.

These are just the facts. Not an indictment. None of this makes Simon's intentions, nor those of his writing staff, which included few Black writers, vicious. Much of what we see in *The Wire* is very noble. It's hard to miss Simon's idealism. There is no question that he is in search of truth and human decency, even when the show seems to beg us to keep forgiving Jimmy McNulty's bad behavior. The main problem in my eyes is that we haven't all gotten to fully discuss *The Wire*—its triumphs and its failures. Instead, White men have largely dominated criticism of *The Wire*. And while what they see is not invalid, it is incomplete. They bring a specific set of eyes to the job, and so do we.

That we, as in Black writers, also have something to say, to borrow from Andre 3000. So I wanted to assemble a group of writers, Black writers, who would share their perspectives on the impactful series. I did not want the jargon typically found in these assessments. Instead, I wanted people, especially those who watched *The Wire* in real time, when it received very little outside praise (contrary to what many news outlets reported when covering Michael K. Williams's unexpected death), to share what they saw and, perhaps, even continue to see in the show in their own words. I did not want the emotion stripped away. For some, *The Wire* may be foreign territory. For people like myself, there are truths in the show that maybe Simon himself did not see coming. That's what the three "Parts of the Familiar" writers I mentioned earlier reference.

And speaking of the familiar, how could we not acknowledge Michael K. Williams in a big way? So Part 4, "The Incredible Lightness of Being Omar and Michael K. Williams," does just that. Writer Scott Wilson shares how Williams's role as Omar personally opened him up to a community he had previously not seen. And I share insights from my three interviews with Williams. I can't claim that I knew him, but I do know that his work matters, and I hope those conversations shed light on why.

The most controversial part of this book will probably be Part 2,

Omar (Michael K. Williams) shares a bench with his adviser, Butchie (S. Robert Morgan). Photo courtesy of HBO

"Baltimore vs. *The Wire*," which is why I am addressing it last. Writers Michael A. Gonzales, Ericka Blount Danois, and Julia Chance, who know Baltimore far more intimately than I do, offer different insights and provide critiques only folks who have lived in a city could. I have met more than a few Baltimore folks who, like that director, didn't watch the show. When I interviewed the young ladies of the documentary *Step*, who found their outlet forming and maintaining their step team, about their experiences navigating Baltimore, they were very clear about not wanting people to think Baltimore is *The Wire*. So there was absolutely no way to not address the very real elephant in this room.

Constructive criticism does indeed have its place, especially when it comes from those with significant ties to the city in question or even the hardscrabble realities of the show. For those who believe the show is indeed perfect, this might be a bitter pill to swallow. However, Black Lives Matter has freed us in a sense, allowing us to have more real conversations about a lot of things. I, for one, watched and enjoyed *The Wire* but remain bothered by how Black girls in the hood are presented in contrast to their male counterparts. So we can put a show under a microscope, as *Cracking The Wire During Black Lives Matter* does, and still admire it. Some, even after striking it with body blows, love *The Wire* and hail it as the best TV show ever.

So yes, I can see how the director could have trouble getting past the White gaze he's found inescapable in his attempts to watch *The Wire*. But I also see how the publicist still watches the show daily in the 2020s and gets lessons from it. Different lenses see different things. I am just so happy to have the conversation!

Sonja Sohn's Kima Greggs: a trailblazing character. Photo courtesy of HBO

PART 1

Pieces of the Familiar

Introductory Overview

By Ronda Racha Penrice

In "Target," the very first episode of *The Wire*, the camera pans past three streams of blood on the pavement before angling up to the body from which it oozes. It then hits Detective Jimmy McNulty (Dominic West) as he is speaking to a witness who knew the victim as Snot or Snot Boogie. As the man on the stoop informs McNulty that Snot was basically killed for something that was a known pattern—stealing money from craps games in the alley—his death becomes more personal as we realize that he mattered to somebody.

As simple as that concept sounds, crime dramas have typically denied this little bit of humanity to its Black characters. Too often they are dead and nameless, relegated to just Thug Number One or Number Two. But these people do matter to somebody. Just not enough to everybody. The stories of *The Wire* aren't just great tales to some people. For those who have come through the fire, there are pieces of the familiar that resonate in ways those uninitiated can't relate to. Representation is powerful. Seeing a glimpse of something you know, especially on a screen where your very existence, your humanity, has been denied, is powerful. *The Wire*, like other shows, was not perfect, but it was a start. Would 50 Cent have a *Power*verse on Starz had there not been a *Wire*?

These three essays acknowledge what so many who had long been unheard and unseen found in a TV show. Harlem native Odell Hall provides a compelling overview as to why *The Wire* so immediately resonated, while also providing the context in which the show lives in "*The Wire* and the Games We Play." Memphis-born writer and editor Sheree Renée Thomas exits her Afrofuturistic universe largely filled with sci-fi and fantasy and crashes back to earth, sharing how *The Wire* captures the very real impact drug addiction had on her own family. And then there is Atlanta native Ed Adams, whose "The Otherlove of Omar Little" digs far beyond LGBTQ representation. For him, Michael K. Williams's Omar is no archetype; he's beyond real and very personal.

These are portraits that typically get washed away in jargon, that are stripped of that emotional impact and connection that make *The Wire* so real. What's fiction for some is indeed real life for others. A show that can reach both is indeed golden. Black folks I know from more privileged backgrounds, for which the circumstances and setting of *The Wire* are indeed foreign, have shared that the show gave them some understanding of what poor, working-class Black people might face. With so much stacked against some of us, it's hard to imagine how they make it through it all. These writers, like *The Wire* itself, don't answer why things are the way they are, but they do give us a sense of not just the challenges, but also of how it feels to be seen and why it's so necessary.

\

1

The Wire and the Games We Play

By Odell Hall

Political intrigue. High-minded drama. In the universe of modern mass media, you would be hard-pressed to see such stories with Black Americans at the center of the tale. Our lot, particularly in television, is always coupled with struggle and failure. Always the victim and never the victor.

When there is any level of dignity or majesty afforded to Black people, it is Wakanda or Zamunda. Or we are allegorized as lions or other cartoons. We are the "magical negroes," existing solely to further the story of some hapless White man or woman, helping them find themselves in time to save the day.

Tony Soprano was a racist, murderous sociopath, and yet he was afforded a sympathetic view through the familiar lens of family dysfunction. We find "lovable" White characters in Jeffrey Dean Morgan's post-apocalypse Negan on *The Walking Dead*—in the gilded, spoiled, and incestuous Jaime Lannister from *Game of Thrones*.

But there ain't no Westeros for niggas. Our kingdoms exist only in prison or on the street. Until some savior wants to dance us out of the ghetto or coach our basketball team while persuading us that our lives have meaning. Sometimes we luck out on *Law & Order: SVU* and an unarmed Black man is shot and killed by police. Then, we get a panoramic view of the Black community, along with a rabble-rousing reverend for good measure. Bonus points for the exceptional Andre Braugher's guest appearances in other episodes as powerhouse defense attorney Bayard Ellis.

When *The Wire* debuted in 2002, it introduced a different level of Black humanity to television. Shakespearean-level drama with a predominantly Black cast in a major American city. Wars of word and wit. Opposing armies employing intelligence and counterintelligence. There was betrayal of the highest order and the self-sacrifice of soldiers willing to lay down their lives. *The Wire* featured both a rogue gay antihero stickup artist and a drug dealer taking business school classes.

There were rules of engagement, including a gentleman's agreement to cease hostilities on Sundays. An annual basketball armistice. They employed children like in a modern-day Crusades in the name of a never-ending turf war. And Black people were at the heart of it all. Not as gold-chained, gold-toothed henchmen credited as Thug #1. But Omar. Stringer. Avon. Proposition Joe. The sociopaths you could love.

Neither the cops nor the crooks were the heroes of *The Wire*. The show was devoid of the usual childish notions of good and evil, which allowed the viewers to take sides based on the people rather than position. No superpredators and no Captain Americas. This allowed for an intimacy with the Black characters that isn't possible in standard police procedurals.

The Wire's police were motivated not by some righteous altruism, but by a very real cat-and-mouse game in which they tried to prove themselves smarter than the street criminals they chased. There is no Eliot Ness, Olivia Benson, Leroy Gibbs, or any other law-enforcement character with some delusion of justice.

The police were dysfunctional as well: chain-of-command, ego-driven stupidity, organizational failures of varying degrees (Hamsterdam?), and, of course, Jimmy McNulty, a barely functioning alcoholic who had his sons playing hide-and-go-seek with a man suspected of being a drug kingpin. And that's before McNulty manufactured a serial-killer hoax to keep his case going.

The Wire resonated in every hood in America. We knew people like these characters and their capacity to do enormous things. But they were locked out and locked up. If given access, they had the talent, the charisma, and the drive to have been successful. Instead, they sought to get over before they went under. And in varying degrees the story of *The Wire* is the story of America. In a similar manner to how *The Cosby Show* framed Black life as American life, *The Wire* presented Black Americans desiring what all Americans want: a chance to win the game.

The show's immersive characters, cinematography, and language conjured a new world to the uninformed. West Baltimore is as much a character as anyone or anything else. From the children, its corners and row houses, and its institutions right down to the junkies and the language, *The Wire* required no suspension of disbelief. The work was done to ensure proximity to reality. Perhaps as close as any modern fiction has dared to go.

Baltimore's institutions (the schools, the justice system, the ports, and even its [White] news media) were given equal organizational footing to the drug trade. Each came with its inescapable truths and its rules, politics, and pitfalls to navigate. This in effect did much to humanize the drug trade. *The Wire* illustrated that crime was not the easy way out for the underclass. Instead, it was the ONLY way out for many of them.

The long-form narrative enabled legitimate character development. Viewers were spoon-fed morsels of each so that the unfamiliar could get summarily hip. If you didn't know the streets, the Barksdale Org was your entry. Avon and Stringer grew up together and established it together. But as the show progressed, it became clear that Avon viewed it as the family business, while the streets were simply a business opportunity for Stringer.

We were introduced to how those seemingly small differences led to drastically different approaches to the same business and ultimately a tragic dissolution of their partnership. Stringer called the police on Avon. Avon called Brother Mouzone on Stringer. The game exacted

The dapper Stringer Bell (Idris Elba) intimidates even in a business suit.
Photo courtesy of HBO

consequences for them both.

There is the corruption of children and their co-option toward the continuance of the "Crack Crusades." Wallace's complicity in the murder of Omar's lover ultimately wracked him with enough guilt for him to cooperate with police: a cardinal street sin. His love for the only home and friends he knew led to his foolhardy return and ultimate murder by those same friends.

The Wire put generational maladies on full display as Wee-Bey Brice's son Namond was urged by his mother to continue participation in the drug trade. But Wee-Bey from prison proved to be a better father to his son than when he was free, exhorting Namond's mother to free the boy from that cycle. And we bore witness to the humanity of the coldest of killers.

Omar Little was cut down with no respect as the next generation of poisoned children stood in line to replace their counterparts, reminding us to see that no one had immunity from the game's consequences and that not all endings were poetic.

We even saw Poot, who lost all his friends to the streets, who earned his stripes by murdering his childhood friend Wallace, decide that enough was enough after the violent murder of Bodie. An unlikely survivor, he quit the streets, just walked away, and got a regular job.

We were introduced to children who were prisoners of both their environment and their families. They fought to go to school. They fought to avoid the gangs. And when they lost those fights, they sought to retain whatever humanity they could and found the camaraderie and protection they could not find at home. These beautiful, broken Black children were failed by every single institution in Baltimore, and yet they still persevered like weeds, contending with mighty oak trees for resources and water.

As the police surveilled the drug trade, we watched Baltimore perpetually teeter on the brink of collapse, held in equilibrium solely by the continued interplay of its institutions both illicit and legit. Their interdependence proved necessary for the city's continued yet suboptimal survival.

If you believe that policing should evolve beyond a war on drugs toward actually addressing the real needs of citizens, then it was obvious that the school system was inept. That recognition would require the news to reassign its villains. The city and surrounding business community would have to also serve *all* of Baltimore.

Black people fueled *The Wire*. They were not just hapless victims shuttled between institutions in a perpetual cipher of failure. They were Baltimore's lifeblood, propping up the economy and the general welfare of the municipality. The lives that mattered most yet considered the least.

The best part of the show was the absence of the idea that it will all get better, that there was light at the end of the tunnel. In the end, the drugs still moved, the stickup kids still stuck, and the bodies still dropped. The paper still published, the politicians still self-served and stole, and the schools still failed their charges. And above all, the police still waged war instead of protecting and serving.

So, when we watched *The Wire*, we knew Black people were essential to the story, and not only diversity garnish. We saw both our violence and our vulnerability. Our malice and our mercy. The raising of armies and the waging of wars. The parlay of our generals and the struggle of street soldiers. The funding of those wars and the maintenance of supply chains as well as the forming of alliances. The framing of the drug trade as an institution gave the people of *The Wire* their own fiefdom. We got our Westeros.

But more importantly, Black people had a real level of agency. We were calculating, moving people with real families and dreams and motivations. We won some. We lost some. Street people regularly outwitted the police, while Stringer, the businessman, was taken for bread by a politician. Sheeeiit.

Deals were made. Marlo, the force of nature, negotiated himself freedom and riches but found himself locked out of the game. Prop Joe, who saw everything as a transaction, ended up on the wrong side of the ledger. The Barksdale Org went under, Marlo's murderous crew was left rudderless, and Slim Charles, perhaps the only person totally true to the game, actually won the street Game of Thrones.

The game never stops. *The Wire* at least allowed us to play.

ϡ

ODELL HALL is a Harlem-born, Charlotte-based writer, podcaster, and editor whose work has appeared in *SXSW Magazine*, AllHipHop.com, Planetill.com, *Love Peace & Slander*, and various other outlets. His cultural observations have run the gamut of music, politics, economics, society, and technology, across various media. In addition, he is cohost of the podcasts *Firing Squad Radio* and *Illside Radio* and a frequent guest on Vocalo Radio's *Weekend Gabe Show*. His publishing company, Kagyai-Hall Publishing, is dedicated to chronicling the journeys and telling the stories of Black people across the diaspora.

2

Walking *The Wire*

By Sheree Renée Thomas

The first time I tried to watch *The Wire*, I turned it off; didn't want to see another pile of unmourned Black bodies desecrating a block. Back then I knew too well how Black lives that bled onto cracked concrete were all just backdrop, set pieces in a larger plot that neither served nor saved us. Didn't want to see the disregard on another TV screen when that disregard did not reflect reality. What I knew was what too many others knew: every other family who had lost someone for a time or forever to drug addiction or the underground drug economy. For me, the fetishized fiction of glorified cops and heartless dope slangers and gangbangers was entertainment some audiences could ill afford. I knew what every hollow-eyed, grief-stricken child, sister, brother, mother, father knew. That behind every blood-stained white tee, the ubiquitous "wife beater" visible on any hot day in the 'hood, was a whole person, a human life whom someone, somewhere, once loved and still does.

Sensationalized and sanitized, the popular television police procedurals that dramatized the war on drugs did not show what we all knew to be inalienably true, that the war on drugs was a euphemism for the never-ending war on Black people in America. For all the faux dichotomies of heroism and nihilism, the public performance of law and order did not show the true costs, the real body count, the ones buried below ground and the ones grieving above. *Starsky & Hutch, Kojak, Hill Street Blues, NYPD Blue, Law & Order, Cops*, etc. did not show the true costs of loss.

And what was lost?

A life or just time—years, decades even, birthdays and yearly report cards, perfect attendance and honor rolls, time marked by inches and old shoes that don't fit, ridiculous hairstyles and fashions swept away by new trends, meals eaten or missed, shared memories that no longer exist—lives and time that were taken that cannot be returned.

I turned *The Wire* off wondering, how can a TV show capture this?

*

My father, a veteran and a highly creative garage inventor, built epic sound machines and speakers for his own listening pleasure. I remember the pride in his eyes, the sheer joy when he and my mother would listen to album after album, each night filled with their singing, the soundtrack of my early youth. Born of a proud and hardworking people unafraid to dream ambitiously for a future he would not live to fully see, my father was not born to be a street soldier or a dope fiend. He had been raised by loving elders whose wood-paneled walls held the gilded faces of hope and history. Jesus Christ and Rev. Dr. King resided stoically alongside Kennedy and the sepia-stained photos of distant relatives and close kin whose eyes carried pain steeped in shadows rarely discussed.

Back then, Black death was a reality on the North Memphis streets, but it was not yet the daily televised entertainment it would become beyond the news. My grandmother loved me in the same three-room house in which she loved and raised my father, the precocious child of neighbors she worked with. The framed oil paintings and vintage photos that stared down at me as a child were the same ones that watched my father, a small, round-headed boy, as he sat nibbling sardine salad and Keebler's crackers with lemonade on a faded Coca-Cola breakfast tray. He sat and did his homework on the same dark velvet, cobalt blue couch that I scratched and rubbed when I was nervous or bored or hungry or just full of wonder, thinking widely, being still.

The brown wood television set that streamed through the darkness of Grandmama's living room was the same window into a world that my father traveled through. Pictures of who and what we could be, mixed with the stories and adventures, the comedies and the B-movie horrors that filled the air. Horror movies were our favorites—wild-eyed zombies, spooks, and phantoms, the dispossessed. In many of them were unspoken ideas of Blackness, of otherness, complicated narratives that we struggled to unpack. Never did I imagine, never did he imagine that some of the stories, some of those horrors might come true.

I avoided *The Wire* the way I had avoided drugs in my own life coming of age, stealthily disappearing like the black-caped magician in the high-top hat we used to watch on weekends. I didn't want to become one of the corner store fiends, whose bloodshot eyes and cocaine-carved cheekbones hinted at the chaos beneath their skin. *Don't save her, she don't want to be saved,* was the Project Pat refrain I feared could someday follow me if I didn't vigilantly "Just Say No." After all, I had already lost my favorite aunt to the ravages of the unknown, a stunning, incomprehensible loss that wounds to this day. If someone as vibrant, brave, beautiful, and unapologetically brilliant as she could disappear without a trace, life snatched just from "partying," then what could happen to me?

I had never been lucky, could never hope to be as beautiful. The best I had was some "book sense," and was still trying to catch up with common sense. If drugs could take some of the most brilliant people whom I knew in my life, my favorite aunt, still missing, and my beloved father, returned to us whole, then what could it do to me, what wouldn't it do to me? So I became the square at the club, the designated driver who couldn't drive, the one who would laugh and smile and dance all around you while watching warily as you got completely fucked up. I'd sip a little drink, mostly something sweet because alcohol tasted like gasoline to me, and keep it moving. I did not have time to be the refrain on the corner, walking on a wire, *Don't save her, she don't want to be saved.* But I vowed to save myself. I vowed that would never happen to me.

Many years after *The Wire*'s last season, after I was well past grieving the time we lost with my father, after we had been reunited to make new memories, a friend asked me if I had seen his favorite show. One of the show's most loved actors was starring in another show, *Boardwalk Empire*, and everyone referred to him not by his born, given name but by his most infamous character's name, Omar.

I said what I always said, that I had never seen an episode of the show all the way through, that it had been unbearable for me. He advised that I skip Seasons 1 and 2. "The first one is cops and robbers, introducing the players. Second one is some Greeks on the docks, but Season 3, that shit's gonna get you.

"They never won an award, the biggest robbery of a show that was about hustling and robbin'."

He told me *The Wire* was the best thing ever to appear on television. Cynicism does not express the skepticism that I felt when he said that. What about seeing Black teens cornered in a dangerous, violent world would be so compelling, would garner such high praise, with folks declaring it revelatory and life changing?

It wasn't until I met Bubbles and those children, the heartbreaking, scrappy, vulnerable, fiercely intelligent, resilient children, like Michael and Duquan "Dukie" Weems, that my hardness against this series began to crack. I confess that I don't recall ever seeing actor Andre Royo perform any character that would be deemed "respectable" until perhaps his appearance as a lawyer on *Empire*. But respectability politics aside, Royo's heart-wrenching and comical performance became the touchstone that kept me glued to the screen, even when I wanted to turn away. The fact that he was never even nominated for his work just echoed for me the kind of disrespect and disregard that the real Reginald "Bubbles" Cousinses experience in the world.

I watched this man with his disheveled hair, ill-fitting clothes, open sores and swollen gums, and wounds, so many wounds on his body, face, skin, the desperation and powerlessness in his eyes, and I worried, and I wept. No one had told me or my younger brothers that the reason my father disappeared for those years was not because he had stopped loving us, but it was because he did not want us to see him after he had stopped loving himself. That he had become addicted to drugs, body and mind snatched up by a force that he had not anticipated overpowering his own good nature and will, he who had been one of the chosen ones, the bright and shining successful ones in a city of heartbreak and hard times. Good job, home, beautiful wife, healthy kids, moving on up with disposable income and time to party and play. Like it did so many others, partying on the scene had done him in, but young as we were, we didn't know it. And apparently, neither he nor our loved ones wanted us to know it. So, the odd, erratic behavior, the disappearances, the strange outings that seemed at first like family bonding time but were actually fronts, and the broken promises, missed meetings once my mom had enough and moved us away so we wouldn't see how far he'd fallen. All the things I had come to learn later were the very things I did not wish to watch casually as entertainment in a TV show. Before I felt healed enough to experience *The Wire*, it was David Simon's first iteration of this struggle, *The Corner*, that captured my attention, despite my wariness. It was the closest any series that I had seen that attempted to show the destruction of whole Black families as a result of the mass drug addiction had come to depicting the hidden and ugly truth of what is now, decades and untold numbers of devastated families later, finally being treated like the health crisis it is.

I shook my head, heartsick over Bubbles's failed attempts in Season 4 to re-create with young Sherrod the family and trust he lost from his own addiction. When his desperate revenge plot to finally stop the man who had repeatedly beaten and robbed him backfired, I grieved as Bubbles mourned another harrowing choice with terrifying consequences. As I watched these riveting twists of fate, I was struck by who was missing from the scenes of death, the families who cried and mourned and never stopped loving or missing the missing. As Bubbles and each child in turn struggled to navigate the brutal and violent streets, their daily lives caught in a cycle of chaos, danger, and loss, I sent up prayers of thanks for all those known and unknown heroes who kept my father alive long enough to fight his own addiction and return his body, spirit, and mind back whole to us. Episode after episode, I scanned the faces of the extras, the background, and looked for the hope of happy endings too often denied us. In the stories where good is pitted against evil, the sociopolitical forces that shape the lives of those who occupy the corners of the war on drugs streets are often left invisible and unchallenged. We are told that war is inevitable and that all of its "collateral damage" is an acceptable loss, that we should hope only for small victories, a life that does not end in homicide or prison.

Seeing Bubbles's sister finally trust him enough again to allow him back into her home was a journey that spoke to some of that hope. It reminded me of my father's courageous journey back to health and love, and all the work and time and trading of hard memories that were needed to arrive at a place of peace and forgiveness. I wanted

Bubbles (Andre Royo) was based on a real-life CI of the same name who died of AIDS. Photo courtesy of HBO

young, bright, caring Dukie, like Bubbles and Namond, who found safe haven with Major Colvin and his wife, to have his version of a hopeful way out. Although it is never quite clear what addiction plagued Dukie's parents, audiences are clear on the cruel circumstances that left him homeless, abandoned by his family like the discarded clothes and pressed wood furniture Dukie and his friends found on the sidewalk after the family's eviction.

Dukie's abandonment showed the instability and nomadic nature of poverty and addiction. That he was left without so much as a forwarding address or a number showed just how precarious and isolated he was. Beyond his friends, who struggled against their own dysfunctional storylines, Dukie had only one person to take an interest in him, and that was as long as it was convenient. Jermaine Crawford's breathtaking performance during an arc that sent him on a path that perhaps paralleled Bubbles's entrée into a life of addiction disrupted television's (and the world's) false hero narratives surrounding cops and educators working with "at-risk" communities.

Jermaine Crawford gives a "breathtaking performance" as Dukie, a member of Season 4's Fayette Mafia Crew. Photo courtesy of HBO

Long before coverage of police brutality and protests became a daily if not weekly staple of the news, I didn't want to watch *The Wire* because I feared we all had grown desensitized to Black suffering. From the era of minstrelsy, in stereotypical advertisements and media, throughout the history of television, we have been taught to laugh at, applaud, and ignore Black trauma and death. The negative treatment of Black bodies and lives on and off the screen is normalized, our suffering rationalized. It is always our fault, always justified. Our damage is not only acceptable but profitable. But what the writers and cast of *The Wire* were able to do, over five seasons, is raise a mirror to and challenge the distorted representations of Black people, puncture a hole in the hardened silence and idolatry surrounding the Blue Shield, render ridiculous the arguments against police accountability and the notion of treating drug addiction as a criminal offense rather than a health epidemic, and make clearer the connection between direct and indirect public policy on Black lives.

Though painful to watch, both *The Corner* and *The Wire* bear witness to what so many families witnessed in their own lives, beyond the screens. They showcase the insanity, the futility, and the hope-shattering injustice of the current policy system and drug policy in America. Even a halfway decent, figuring-it-out cop like Sergeant Ellis Carver couldn't save Randy, a good child who had no affiliations with gangs, drugs, or other crime. He was just a poor child with no stable family to support him. Season 5 revealed the depths and tragedy of that sad reality, and showed that the severe poverty and destabilization in Randy's community were not due to "bad culture" or a lack of policing.

Seeing on the screen all the many ways Black families and communities are devastated and failed by public policy reminded me that while thankfully my own father was saved, there are still so many of our loved ones who are not. Watching the courageous storytelling of *The Wire* reminded me of the priceless blessing that is my family, survivors of an endless war. With an uncommon attention to detail, natural dialogue, and an appreciation of those most vulnerable, most at stake, the celebrated though shamefully not awarded series reveals that the futile war on drugs federal policy is not mere entertainment, but a choice. That is, unless we, as a society, challenge the destructive inherited systems and narratives of this war, the stories we tell each other about who deserves mercy and who deserves suffering and pain, many more fathers, mothers, brothers, sisters, and children will remain caught out there, walking the wire, by our choice.

❧

SHEREE RENÉE THOMAS is an award-winning fiction writer, poet, and editor. Her work is inspired by myth and folklore, natural science, and the genius of Mississippi Delta culture. *Nine Bar Blues: Stories from an Ancient Future* (Third Man Books, 2020), her fiction collection, was a 2021 Finalist for the Locus, Ignyte, and World Fantasy Award for Year's Best Collection. She is also the author of two hybrid collections, *Sleeping Under the Tree of Life* (Aqueduct Press, 2016), longlisted for the 2016 Otherwise Award and honored with a *Publishers Weekly* starred review, and *Shotgun Lullabies* (Aqueduct, 2011). She edited the two-time World Fantasy-winning groundbreaking black speculative fiction anthology *Dark Matter* and was the first to introduce W. E. B. Du Bois's science fiction short stories. Her work is widely anthologized and appears in Marvel's *Black Panther: Tales of Wakanda*, edited by Jesse J. Holland (Titan, 2021), and *The Big Book of Modern Fantasy*, edited by Ann and Jeff VanderMeer (Vintage, 2020). She is the editor of *The Magazine of Fantasy & Science Fiction*, founded in 1949, and is the associate editor of *Obsidian*, founded in 1975. She was recently honored as a 2020 World Fantasy Award Finalist in the Special Award— Professional category for contributions to the genre. Visit www.shereereneethomas.com

3

The "Otherlove" of Omar Little

By Ed Adams

I've always considered myself a romantic—hopelessly so, actually. And being a Black man who is a romantic in America? Well, it has its moments.

There's this expectation, you see. You're born into an archetype. From early on, you are told in no uncertain terms you're supposed to be a buck, a stud of Mandingo proportion, full of virility and machismo. At seven or eight years old, you may not even know the title. You just know people call you handsome and tell you "You're going to be a ladies' man" or, better yet, "a heartbreaker."

You're also taught to be hardcore. You are told to speak up and speak your mind and no crying. It's drilled into you to never back down, and learn how to hold your own, or, in simple translation, to give as much as you get when in a fight or backed in a corner.

The worst thing growing up as a young Black boy was to be labeled a punk. That meant you were outside—an other, a pariah. A traitor to your birthright, a walking blight in colored skin. For some brothers out there, it's a scar you either learn to live with or hide—being visible and invisible at the same time. Such is the conundrum. The extra weight some boys bear along with the heft of their Black skin . . . and we just deal with it.

Which brings me to *The Wire* and its favorite son, Omar Little.

Omar is probably one of the most original characters to ever grace our television screens. Part gangster, part Robin Hood, Omar's creed is equally yoked by his swagger and unapologetic bravado. He represents something we hadn't seen in film or television aside from maybe Cleo in the film *Set It Off.* A man forged in the streets, honed to be sharper than a razor's edge to stake his claim in the game.

But there's something else Omar brings to *The Wire*, and if you're not careful, you'll definitely miss it. Among the mafioso-style street jargon and dealer rhetoric, there is no passion–no love quartered nor offered from Avon, Stringer, nor their minions. They are hard, coded to be, as expected, the Black thugs and bucks we expect them to be. Even if you shift to see just where the police fit into this melee, mostly on the machinations of Jimmy McNulty and his posse, it's more of the same tropes in the game of chess played out methodically and with purpose, but lacks that singular thing that would normally tug at you. That is until Omar gives it to you.

Watching Omar with his boyfriends Brandon, Dante, and Renaldo, openly gay and sharing those moments from the streets to the sheets, was glorious. Watching them, the connection was honey—sweet and sticky, captivating and hard to forget the delicious taste of it all. Even seeing him with his warm almost surrogate father, Butchie, and at times with his crew was exactly what the world needed to see on a show like this. I've been calling it "otherlove" for a while now. That nontraditional, familiar feeling that sits just on the periphery of expected and accepted. And with this show, we ingested each moment and were for once satisfied.

Omar was the topic of discussion among friends often as we'd recap the episodes. Most times we'd laugh; no words needed to be said. We felt a shared warmth from our smiles and giggles from one other to another, and it felt so good to be in and of that moment.

For me it mattered because I didn't grow up in the mean streets of Baltimore and I have no drug stories to tell as part of my upbringing. But I knew some Omars, those people—the others, the lovely souls that showed me just what otherlove is all about.

My first true understanding of that other thing came from my cousin. To protect his name, I'll just call him D. His mother sent him from Birmingham to stay with us in Atlanta after he had gotten into some trouble. We never knew exactly what trouble he had gotten himself into, but she hoped a fresh start in a new city would straighten him out. But it didn't.

D wouldn't change. He'd disappear for hours at a time and come home at the crack of dawn. He never found a job but always had money. It was jarring for my folks, and after a month or so of his ways, they put him out. He moved into an apartment a couple of blocks away, and he was still welcomed to our table for dinner even though he wasn't welcomed to spend the night. But he rarely came.

Whenever he stopped by, he'd always extend an invitation to me to come over. At that time, I felt like I wasn't myself most days—I was hiding from the world and felt terrified to confront the notion that I wasn't normal, that I was an other and didn't belong. So my curiosity got the better of me and I decided to take my cousin up on his invite, to see if his different was close to or the same as my own. I knocked and a stranger opened the door. He had an early field of cornrows atop his head, half of them still in an Afro with a comb stuck within a part. He looked menacing and intimidating.

"Can I help you?" he said.

I literally gulped and looked at the number on the door. *Maybe I'm at the wrong place*, I thought. *Maybe this isn't where I'm supposed to be.*" I mustered enough courage to ask, "Is D here?" Thinking back, I sound so mousy in my head. Somehow he knew I had to be his cousin, so he invited me in. I walked in the living room. The carpet was clean, but I saw drink stains and ashtrays all over the floor. My host walked to the sofa and sat on the floor position between the legs of a tall, lanky guy with long Jheri curls like Michael Jackson. He looked at me, and my host (I never got his name, honestly) introduced me as D's cousin, and then invited me to take a seat. I sat on one of the two large velour beige sofas, making myself as small as I could be.

"D, your cousin is here!" he shouted.

To me it felt as if people sprung from the ether. Two guys came from a bedroom and peeked to see who had come calling. They wore wifebeaters and basketball shorts, both holding cigarettes, one holding a bottle. They said hi, then went back to their room. I don't know who they were expecting, but it was clear I didn't hold their interest. Another guy came from another room and said, "Your cousin is in the shower; he'll be out in a minute." He had kind eyes and offered me something to drink. I was too afraid to say no and was ushered into the kitchen. Sitting there were four other guys, playing spades, smoking joints, and drinking beer. I was introduced and they gave a collective "Sup?" I gave a head nod to signify I was just as cool, just as chill as they were. I was offered some Kool-Aid from a Tupperware pitcher and went back to my space on the sofa. I listened to them talk about this and that. It felt trivial and important at the same time. I didn't know much about the world they came from, and I tried my best to decipher every word. But I couldn't. I didn't know these people or places they'd talk about. I only got the sense that they were meeting up later that night.

My cousin finally appeared, sauntering out wearing a pink silk robe loosely tied around his waist. His only other clothing was a pair of cotton briefs that he was obviously comfortable in. His roommates seemed accustomed to his shocking and garish garb. My face must have been a bundle of confused knots, because he smiled and said, "What, you don't like my robe?" I was too embarrassed to say anything but caught myself enough not to lose my cool and said, "It's alright. Just never seen a guy wear pink before." He and his friends laughed at me, and I blushed.

After that, he sat next to me and we talked as cousins do. We caught up and he fixed me something to eat. The room and the people in it became more familiar, and I was let into some of the inside jokes that had originally floated high above my head. For the first time, I saw— no, knew—what other was and just how wonderful and special it is.

That day I learned that otherlove is how our body sustains itself by establishing new connections when others are shunted, a valuable lesson for a high school kid to understand.

After my cousin walked me home, my parents forbade me from visiting D at his apartment again. They never explained why to me, and D stopped coming over as well. The only time I'd see him was at the train station when I got off late from work. My mom would call him, and he'd meet me at the station to walk me home. As always, he would be waiting for me with a cigarette in one hand and a bottle wrapped in a paper bag in the other. He was surrounded by his housemates, and they would walk me home. I walked behind them and again tried to decipher their conversations. People would look at the gang of us making our way through the neighborhood late night. Sometimes I could feel the eyes on us and the cold glaring air of disgust. But nobody would say a word; people didn't fuck with them. I don't know if they had a rep, but when we walked past others, they were as rambunctious as ever, while others stared as quiet as church mice. As we got close to my home, they'd see me off from the corner with a quick wave, never putting a foot on my street.

I never shared with my folks the things I heard on those nights or how special that group made me feel, but I still carry that feeling, that knowing other otherness, with me to this day. And I saw this exact same otherlove between Omar and Brandon in Season 1. And I felt the pain and loss after Brandon's broken body was set on display.

As the show continued, I saw more facets of Omar's other. I saw his close connection to Butchie and his affection with Dante. I watched with anticipation as our whistling Robin Hood morphed into Edmond Dantès of *The Count of Monte Cristo* and Javert of *Les Misérables* to rescue his love Dante, and cheered when he exacted his revenge on Avon, Stringer, and Marlo.

When David Simon created Omar, an intended throwaway paradox of a character with so much bravado he describes himself in the third person, never in his wildest imagination could he have realized he would become bigger than the series itself.

Omar is the heart of the series and represents the hidden parts of the game that thrive beyond the drug wheeling and dealing. As much as the show desperately tried to make Jimmy McNulty the heart of *The Wire*, Omar stole ours. He represents the family, friends, neighbors we know who embrace their lifestyle in their own unique way. Yes, in some Black communities this notion of self-awareness and self-expression is still taboo and definitely off topic. But I feel seeing Omar, this beautifully principled Black brother who shook up the Baltimore streets while simultaneously handling his own, moved the needle a bit. It made the conversation of other a little easier. It made the tension of hiding otherness a little lighter. And it gave this notion of otherlove a face we could hold onto, cherish, and feel damn good about. He shared his otherlove with us, and we are that much better for it.

ED ADAMS has been culture surfing around Atlanta for over fifteen years. The former award-winning digital manager and film critic for *Creative Loafing Atlanta* has also written for *Huffington Post*, *Living Intown* magazine, *Collider*, and *Essence*, to name a few. He was the lead writer for the Martin Luther King Jr. Inaugural Memorial Gala and The Reverend Joseph Lowery's 90th Birthday Celebration and contributing writer and designer for the stage production *In the Midnight Hour: The Music of Wilson Pickett*. The Atlanta native is a proud member of the African American Film Critics Association (AAFCA), where he has contributed to several projects, including *Kaleidoscope Reviews*, The AAFCA Roundtables, and, as host and producer, *The AAFCA Podcast*.

The Wire was filmed on location in Baltimore. How did the city feel about that?
Photo courtesy of HBO

PART 2

Baltimore vs. *The Wire*

Introductory Overview

By Ronda Racha Penrice

Like most people who watched *The Wire* in real time and those still discovering it now, I am not from Baltimore. I have visited a couple of times and am fortunate to know people from there. The thing that strikes me most about people I have encountered from Baltimore is how many of them hate *The Wire*. Being from Chicago, I kind of get it, because most of the time when I see my city or my people on the screen, they just don't match up. And yes, sometimes we can be protective, defensive even, about our turf. Unfortunately, for Black people, however, what's historically been put on the screen has not represented us. Not in its totality anyway.

To admit this shouldn't suggest anything sinister. It should instead point out the work that can be done. That is what these three writers do. Michael A. Gonzales, in his "B-More or B-Less: Meditations on *The Wire* and Baltimore" essay, takes us into a world that is pre-*Wire* in a sense. It's the world we don't see. A world that he experienced as someone who spent a portion of his upbringing there. Julia Chance, in "Reflections on *The Wire* and the Black Baltimore It Misses," gives us a taste of the rich history that could have enriched *The Wire*. As a self-proclaimed "Wirecologist," Chance observes not just out of love, but also through the very real lens that race in our country matters in Baltimore too. Ericka Blount Danois, in her "Where da Hood At?

The Heartbeat of Baltimore *The Wire* Didn't Detect," perhaps catches so many off guard. After all, "Isn't *The Wire* all about the hood?" some will retort. As Blount Danois demonstrates, the hood is also complex.

Baltimore, according to the Census Bureau, officially became majority Black in 1980. In 2020, forty years later, it was still majority Black. Although Councilman Clarence "Du" Burns technically became the city's first Black mayor when he was elevated to the position in January 1987, after Mayor William Donald Schaefer became Maryland's governor, Kurt Schmoke is the city's first *elected* Black mayor. In 2007, Sheila Dixon became Baltimore's first-ever female mayor, not just Black woman mayor.

The complexity of city governance is one of *The Wire*'s sticking points. One of the things we've discovered, especially in the wake of George Floyd's murder in 2020 and the tragic death of Baltimore's own Freddie Gray in police custody, is that Black governance does not ensure Black safety. In other words, racism is so deeply embedded in our country's DNA that changing the race of the agents doesn't necessarily change the results.

To die-hard fans of *The Wire*, it might hurt to hear some of the truths revealed in some of these essays. But please remember, when a choice is made to represent something real, the expectations and responsibilities are heightened. As fans, we may not always see Baltimore as anything more than the setting of *The Wire*. But for generations of people, Baltimore isn't *The Wire*, it's home. And these three writers underscore that point.

4

B-More or B-Less: Meditations on
The Wire and Baltimore

By Michael A. Gonzales

From the first season of *The Wire*, I had a love/hate relationship with the HBO series some critics and fans anointed "the greatest ever made." Baltimore had been my adopted hometown since 1978, when I moved there from Harlem with my mom and younger brother. It's a city known for crabs, sports teams, and White women who call people "hon." Baltimore has long been the perfect setting for crime narratives, and *The Wire*'s creator, David Simon, a former *Baltimore Sun* reporter, has been behind a few of them. Simon and his producing partner, ex-cop/schoolteacher Ed Burns, crafted five seasons of *The Wire*, filled with brutal storylines that focused on the dog-eat-dog world of the drug "game," as both dealers and cops reference the deadly life of dope fiends and corner boys. "The game's the game," Avon Barksdale said, but it's also as serious as a heart attack. Although *The Wire* went deep into the worlds of the police, politics, dock workers, the school system, and journalism, all roads led to (or away from) the dealers' crumbling row houses, dilapidated housing projects, and trash-strewn alleyways, where rats the size of cats thrived, survived, and multiplied. Years before, Black Baltimore author Jerome Dyson Wright penned the autobiographical crime novel *Poor, Black and in Real Trouble* (1976), which he self-published until selling the reprint rights to Iceberg Slim/Donald Goines publisher Holloway House a few years later, and to me, Wright's title best describes many of the young men and women depicted on *The Wire*.

Even those who weren't poor in material wealth were lacking something: morals, smarts, dignity, or opportunities. The difference is Wright wrote about the mean streets of the fifties and sixties, an era of swinging fists rather than blazing bullets. Back in the seventies, when I moved to a Black Baltimore neighborhood, I saw my share of fights, but I can't recall ever seeing a gun or hearing shots at night. During that time there was still a country essence about the city, a Southern sensibility in the big town. Decades later, those same blocks went beyond mean and became downright deadly.

My old Monroe Street neighborhood transformed from the cool place I once knew, where I hung out with friends and bought cheesesteak sandwiches at a spot called KK's, to a place overrun with decayed housing and vice. It was within that hell, a raging inferno that began blazing two decades before crack cocaine flooded the streets in the 1980s, that so many walked the roughneck path of *The Wire*. Watching the series from day one in the living room of my Brooklyn apartment, I studied the show from several viewpoints, including those of budding crime-fiction writer, cop show aficionado, pop culture critic, and former resident, back when the tag "Charm City" still applied.

Baltimore has prided itself on having a cool slogan and/or moniker since as far back as when Mayor William Donald Schaefer was in office, throughout the 1970s and 1980s. One year another mayor called it "the city that reads." A few years after that, there were billboards and signs encouraging their citizens to "BELIEVE." That campaign, distinguished by wooden bus benches with the sentence "The Greatest City in America" painted in white across the back, was launched in 2002, the same year *The Wire* premiered. Sometimes it seemed as if the city spent more money on its various "Believe" and

"The City That Reads" campaigns, presumably intended to instill city pride, than it did on or in communities that needed help.

For me, as a lover of all things neo-noir, *The Wire* more than satisfied a love of criminal-minded pop culture. Though I thought it pretentious to compare the show to Charles Dickens novels, Herman Melville texts, or Greek tragedies, I admired it as much as I do the pulp novels of Chester Himes and Jim Thompson, the crime films of Sidney Lumet and Steven Soderbergh, and the albums of James Brown and N.W.A.

What drew me to *The Wire* more so than the "gangsta, gangsta" scenarios of dope-slinging and gun-banging was the realness it revealed, especially with the corner boys D'Angelo Barksdale, whose Uncle Avon ran the drug crew, Bodie Broadus, Poot, and Wallace. Though they were young, those boys already behaved like jaded old men. We sometimes got a peek at their vulnerability, disappointments, dreams, memories, and hopes. Unlike other drug dealers in the hood depicted on TV, they weren't merely monsters or demons. They had layers.

Still, in my role as "former resident" who often visited my mother, brother, and friends in the Northwood section of town, I was appalled that television writer/producer David Simon, who hailed from the former "Murder City" of Washington, DC, had created yet another program in Baltimore using Black misery as its jump-off and inspiration. This one came right on the heels of *The Corner*, a miniseries in the same vein, also on HBO.

Though I was drawn to his shows, usually because of the cast and quality, I couldn't help but think there's something problematic about always showing Black folks of Baltimore at their worst. More than a backdrop, the city served as a major character that was as important to the story as Avon Barksdale, Stringer Bell, or Omar Little. Those streets, suites, waterfronts, and buildings belonged to only one town, and I resented Simon for having once again put the negative of my peoples on Front Street.

Simon's rise in television began when his Baltimore-based true-crime book *Homicide: A Year on the Killing Streets* (1991) was turned

The Wire was not David Simon's first look at Baltimore. *Homicide: Life on the Street* aired on NBC in the nineties. Photo courtesy of NBC

into the NBC police procedural *Homicide: Life on the Street*. Produced by Baltimore native son Barry Levinson—a writer/director known for his Charm City-set movies *Diner* (1982), *Tin Men* (1987), *Avalon* (1990), and *Liberty Heights* (1999), as well as the big Hollywood films *Rain Man* (1988) and *Bugsy* (1991)—the series ran from 1993 to 1999. Though the White characters in some of Levinson's movies were working-class and had various issues, none were desolate junkies or criminals from pregentrification neighborhoods Hampden or Pig Town.

A year after *Homicide* was canceled, David Simon wrote and produced his first HBO program, the ghetto drug miniseries (six episodes) *The Corner*. Adapted from another true-crime book, which Simon cowrote with Ed Burns (*The Corner: A Year in the Life of an Inner-City Neighborhood*, 1997), *The Corner* was directed by Charles S. Dutton. More known as an actor on Broadway and in films and television, Dutton was another B-More native son. Raised in the housing project Latrobe Homes in East Baltimore, he was a troubled youth who dropped out of high school and was arrested for murder when he was sixteen. Dutton claimed it was self-defense, that the victim had attacked him with a knife. However, it was while serving a five-year sentence that he discovered the theater arts, which he has turned into an impressive and lucrative career. The brother holds two Tony Award nominations, for roles in the August Wilson plays *Ma Rainey's Black Bottom* (1984) and *The Piano Lesson* (1990), but Dutton didn't become known to the general public until he starred in the Fox TV series *Roc*, depicting the life of a lower-middle-class garbage man living with his wife, jazz musician brother, and retired father in Baltimore; it ran from 1991 to 1994. Considering Dutton's background, he could've created his own hood show, but instead he crafted one featuring the more traditional nuclear family.

Six years later, Dutton made his directorial debut with *The Corner*, a critically acclaimed production that won him a Primetime Emmy for Outstanding Directing for a Miniseries or Movie. Dutton was the only member of the key creative team who grew up in similar surroundings. He even discussed his background in the opener of the first show. It was the success of *The Corner* that led to HBO greenlighting *The Wire*.

While *The Wire* had intriguing storylines, characters, situations, and environments, no matter how much I liked the show, I was pissed off that the Afro representation of my adopted city, where I knew many Black creative artists, social workers, and legit business owners, was once again glorifying the downside of the street.

The "Yo Boys," as my friend Barry Michael Cooper, the journalist and screenwriter who penned *New Jack City* in a Baltimore library, referred to the drug dealers and stickup kids in his award-winning 1986 *Spin* magazine article "In Cold Blood: Baltimore Teen Murders," seemed to be the only subject White filmmakers care about. Despite the deep roots of Black folks in Baltimore, God forbid auteurs or showrunners should ever create a movie or television show where colored folks could also wax nostalgic in the way Barry Levinson and

John Waters, the celebrated writer/director behind *Hairspray* (1988) and *Cry Baby* (1990), have done in their films.

Why couldn't there be a film about the heyday of Pennsylvania Avenue, when the Royal Theatre and the Tijuana Club were in vogue; a biopic on the Black Roller Games women signed to the Baltimore Cats in the 1960s; a documentary about Henry Green Parks, Jr., founder of the Parks Sausages Company, the first Black company traded on the New York Stock Exchange; a book about disco owner Odell Brock, Jr., whose North Avenue club Odell's was known as the Studio 54 of Baltimore; a literary talk show featuring Paul Coates, owner of Black Classic Press and Ta-Nehisi's daddy; or a miniseries about Verda Freeman Welcome, the first African American Maryland state senator?

Not long after *The Wire* aired, people who knew that I considered Baltimore my other home but had never been there themselves inquired, "Is Baltimore *really* like it is on *The Wire*?" That was a question I would be asked many times over the years. In the beginning I'd cop an attitude and snap, "That's not *my* Baltimore. I don't see the people that I know, the kids I went to high school with or their upwardly mobile parents. Hell, when I first moved to Baltimore in 1978, we lived in the hood and it was still nothing like *The Wire*."

Another side of me was angry that yes, there were parts of the city, including my old neighborhood, that had become exactly like *The Wire*. The city had changed considerably since I first moved to 1903 Monroe Street, near North Avenue, in the summer of 1978. Back then I was a fifteen-year-old kid who had recently transplanted from "up top," as some Baltimore folks refer to New York City. It was a lower-middle-class Black neighborhood of row houses, working parents, Black businesses, churches, and plenty of kids.

I had originally come from a New York community that was a multiethnic melting pot, but the Baltimore neighborhood I'd moved to was more segregated than any place I'd ever been. The whitest thing in the neighborhood was the Cloverland Farms Dairy milk processing plant a few blocks from our house. Still, Monroe Street was old-school—kids scrubbed their row house marble steps on Saturday morning, strangers greeted me kindly, and, come Sunday morning, most of our neighbors headed to church.

During my three years across town at Northwestern High School, I witnessed just one fight. Instead of standing out for violence, my classmates were featured in the *Baltimore Sun* for being the most fashionable students in the city. The school was filled with students of various races and socioeconomic statuses, but the Black students stood out. As part of the post-civil rights era, all the Black teens had dreams of being "something" after we graduated, and we had caring teachers who supported, helped, and guided us toward the finish line. At Northwestern, we were offered intern programs, various school organizations, drama workshops, and the school newspaper.

In 1981, when Ronald Reagan took office as America's fortieth president, it all changed. Almost immediately, he began cutting services in the poorer neighborhoods, defunding schools, killing unions, and eliminating jobs in those communities of color that needed them most. These actions, combined with the postindustrial collapse that began in America's factories in the 1970s, were ample indication that the forthcoming decade would be bleak, but when the darkness came, it was pitch-black.

After graduating that same year, I returned to New York for college, but a few times a year I was on Greyhound or Amtrak headed back to Baltimore. Three years later, the powerful drug crack began steadily seeping into our communities, just as it did in my Harlem neighborhood, until one day that bomb exploded, and the potent, smokable cocaine was everywhere. A social worker friend who started working for the state of Maryland in 1980 told me she remembered well how crack had invaded the city, destroying people, property, and pride. "My colleagues and I used to refer to our early years as 'BC,' which stood for Before Crack," she told me. "Before heroin or anything else, it was crack that changed everything."

It has long been believed that the crack epidemic happened because of Reagan and the CIA. While First Lady Nancy Reagan was appearing on talk shows and billboards and in PSAs in which she even sat on Mr. T's lap while encouraging Americans to "just say no" to drugs, her husband's posse was dope dealing in Latin America. Cocaine, once the expensive drug of rock stars and big-time players, became considerably cheaper, and the streets were flooded with the powder that would be turned into crack.

With the drugs came the guns, the gangs, the open street dealing, the violence, and mass incarceration. While most of my friends were spared, we all knew people who took a few blasts and were soon strung out for years. On the other side of that tarnished coin, many of us also knew people who became dealers, living that diamond life until either jail or death took its place. Some people eventually got out of the game, going from crack to Christ, while others eventually weaned themselves from the glass pipe teat or died trying.

Nevertheless, the devastation was already done, and as my social worker friend told me, "Generations were destroyed." The children and grandkids of those generations were the addicts, corner boys, and kingpins who populated the streets on *The Wire*. After the crack days faded, the drugs changed and some streets got worse. Riding Baltimore's public buses, I often saw people nodding out as others just dead-eye stared, showing no emotions. Recently, driving down Monroe Street at night, I noticed that my old house was now boarded up and damn near falling down as a huge rat galloped down the middle of the sidewalk.

While *The Wire* gave many Black actors work, including future stars Idris Elba (Stringer Bell), Michael B. Jordan (Wallace), Michael K. Williams (Omar), and Andre Royo, whose junkie character, Bubbles, was so on point it was scary, behind-the-camera Black people were not as plentiful. Simon and Burns later included other writers, welcoming crime-fiction scribes George Pelecanos, Richard Price, and Dennis Lehane, but only a handful of writers of color contributed to the sixty hours of programming, with Black directors Clark Johnson, Clement Virgo, Ernest Dickerson, Anthony Hemingway, and Seith Mann directing just over 25 percent of the episodes. (Joy Lusco Kecken, a Black woman writer unicorn among *The Wire* writing staff and TV in general at the time, codirected one episode); screenwriter David Mills, an old college friend of Simon's who also cowrote *The Corner*, penned "Soft Eyes," the second episode of the fourth season. A few years before, Mills and I had become cool with each other when he was a music critic at the *Washington Post* and editing a P-Funk fanzine called *Uncut Funk*.

The fourth season concentrated on four neighborhood youngsters: Dukie Weems (Jermaine Crawford), Namond Brice (Julito McCullum), Michael Lee (Tristan Wilds), and Randy Wagstaff (Maestro Harrell), who was my personal favorite. We realize from the first episode of that season, titled "Boys of Summer," that these middle-school kids, living on the edge of gritty street life, could go either way and become fiends and dealers or escape altogether. But at least there was a sense of hope. Having once worked in a homeless shelter populated mostly by single mothers and their children, I had seen preadolescents much like those kids, youngsters who had to take charge of their lives as they literally walked a high wire between evil and good, the streets and school, get high and pass by.

On *The Wire*, none of the kids passed through the jagged edges of the B-More landscape unscathed: Dukie's parents were dopers and drunks; Namond's mother tried to push him into becoming a corner boy like his daddy, Wee-Bey Brice; Michael was dealing with the memory of being sexually abused; and Randy could've gone either way. Among themselves, as with the other "crews" on the show, they formed an unofficial family: taking care of one another, giving advice, defending one another, and following their paths as they made it from day to day. Unlike for the hard rock youths of previous seasons, the "no future" kids slinging on the streets in the first three seasons, there was still an anticipation that they would get out.

In the years since *The Wire* went off the air in 2008, Baltimore has gone through various changes that include certain neighborhoods being revitalized while others have simply gotten worse. As in Chicago or Detroit, the murder rate has steadily risen every year, but there has also been a surge of upwardly mobile Black folks moving here from various parts of the country: filmmakers, writers, lawyers, and musicians. So far there is still no television show about them, but, as Jesse Jackson would say, I'm going to keep hope alive.

ॐ

Harlem native MICHAEL A. GONZALES has written about crime culture for CrimeReads.com, as well as having penned the book column "The Blacklist" for Catapult.co and the "Slept on Soul" music series for Soulhead.com. He is also a former writer at-large for *Vibe* and also has written cover stories for *Essence*, *Latina*, *The Source*, *XXL*, and *Ego Trip*. Gonzales's essays have been published in *Best African American Essays 2010*, edited by Gerald Early and Randall Kennedy, as well as *Baltimore City Paper*, Longreads, the *Paris Review*, *Maggot Brain*, and *Wax Poetics*. He currently lives in Baltimore.

5

Reflections on *The Wire* and the Black Baltimore It Misses

By Julia Chance

It is a sunny summer afternoon and I am standing in the parking lot of The Avenue Bakery in West Baltimore admiring a huge photomontage by artist Stuart Hudgins titled "Our Community's Legacy." I came to see it because my father, Edward Chance, is among dozens of distinguished local leaders pictured, Black men and women from the city's past and present.

The picture with my father first appeared in the *Baltimore Sun* in 1963.

It captures him as the thirty-year-old chairman of the Baltimore branch of CORE (Congress of Racial Equality), standing between Episcopal minister Rev. William Dwyer from New York City and local Methodist minister Rev. Frank Williams. They are embracing in solidarity, mouths parted in song ("I Woke Up This Morning with Freedom on My Mind," according to the original article caption). They are positioned before a Baltimore County Jail cell where they had spent a night for leading the historic march to desegregate Gwynn Oak, an amusement park just outside Northwest Baltimore.

Parren Mitchell, the first African American from Maryland elected to Congress and the first from below the Mason-Dixon Line to be elected to the House of Representatives since Reconstruction in 1898, is pictured in the artwork. So are Kweisi Mfume and Elijah Cummings, who decades later followed in his footsteps. Kurt Schmoke and Sheila Dixon, the first Black man and woman to be mayor of Baltimore, gaze out from atop. Thurgood Marshall appears twice: as the indefatigable NAACP Legal Defense Fund attorney and the groundbreaking Supreme Court justice. Billie Holiday and Cab Calloway are there for good measure. Those two legends weren't born Baltimoreans, but each lived in the city long enough for Black residents to proudly claim them, and both went on to break color barriers in entertainment.

The photomontage stands in the part of West Baltimore depicted on all five seasons of the HBO drama *The Wire*. It's not far from "the pit" where D'Angelo Barksdale slung crack, or the funeral home where Stringer Bell enforced Robert's Rules of Order at crew meetings. It's where Omar Little consulted with his blind banker, Butchie, and Herc, Kima, and Carver rolled up on corner boys. More recently it garnered notoriety after the death of Freddie Gray at the hands of the police. The subsequent uprising that made national news occurred just two months before my visit.

For generations, West Baltimore was a thriving Black community with businesses, churches, and schools, where principals and teachers, doctors and lawyers, domestics and factory workers lived, raised their children, worshipped, shopped, and made a way for themselves in the face of segregation. Some even called it "Baltimore's Harlem."

It was home to the NACCP branch that Eleanor Roosevelt and Martin Luther King visited in the 1950s and 1960s, and all the legendary Black entertainers—from Duke Ellington, Louis Armstrong, and Ella Fitzgerald to the Motown Revue and James Brown—performed at the city's popular Royal Theatre.

Yet I cannot recall any mention of, or reference to, Baltimore's rich Black heritage in the sixty episodes of *The Wire*. Looking back on the series in this era of Black Lives Matter, the 1619 Project, and the so-called reckoning with racism sparked by George Floyd's murder, we can see that the omission of something so essential to understanding the lives of its Black characters makes such an incredible show seem incomplete.

Full disclosure: I am a Wirecologist, the term I jokingly coined to describe my degree of fandom for, and knowledge of, a program that I discovered incidentally. During a period when I didn't have cable TV, my sister taped episodes of *The Sopranos* for me. Once she let the VHS tape run over for about a half hour into the next program, and what I viewed intrigued me a great deal. The pacing was measured, and there was no musical background score. Scenes with Baltimore's iconic brick row houses with white marble steps hinted that it was set in my hometown, and the Black characters looked and talked like people I know. Also, they were way more complex and nuanced than any I had ever watched on television, with Omar adding an element of surprise I would never have considered: a person who robs drug dealers for sport.

Jamie Hector's Marlo Stanfield (left) battled the Barksdale organization for control of the West Baltimore drug trade. Photo courtesy of HBO

Since then, I have watched every episode so many times I have lost count, and I enjoy discussing its Shakespearean themes and story arcs with anyone who will engage me. I get a kick out of the show's many memorable quotes, a testament to the stellar dialogue, and can understand Snoop's Black Baltimore dialect with no need for captions or rewinding.

I have been familiar with David Simon, creator of *The Wire*, since *Homicide: Life on the Street*, a series adapted from his book *Homicide: A Year on the Killing Streets* that aired on NBC in the 1990s. I also watched the 2000 HBO miniseries *The Corner*, a bleak story about drug addiction in Baltimore's Black inner city that Simon adapted with David Mills from a book cowritten by Simon and former Baltimore policeman and schoolteacher Ed Burns. But during *The Wire* I fell down a Simon rabbit hole, wanting to learn more about the man responsible for a show that became my obsession. I voraciously read articles on him and searched the internet for television interviews featuring him on YouTube. I took note of the way he presented: blue-collar style with eloquent speech, salt-of-the-earth everyman and learned scribe. I applauded his take on the corporatization of newspapers and how it is bad for democracy. After all, he was once a newspaper reporter and knew of what he spoke. Hearing him describe *The Wire* as a show about how institutions fail their citizens rather than as a cop show—distinguishing it from the plethora of network police procedurals that have come to define the genre—confirmed for me that I was privy to revolutionary TV storytelling that the masses had not yet discovered. I felt compelled to spread the word, instructing friends to "watch it and tell me what you think."

I even threw a watch party for the final episode in my tiny Brooklyn apartment, complete with *The Wire*-themed swag that I had purchased from the HBO Shop in Manhattan to award as door prizes. An orange prison jumpsuit, to my horror, was my gift-with-purchase.

Yet a lot of my relatives and homies did not share my enthusiasm for *The Wire* at all. They found its emphasis on poor, struggling Black people depressing. Our parents may have been from West Baltimore, but once segregation was outlawed and more housing opportunities opened up for Black people in other areas of the city, they left. Many of us did not have the same connection to our old neighborhoods and, these days, rarely hear positive things about them.

For old-timers like my mother, aunts, and cousins, who remembered West Baltimore's heyday and were distressed by the city's skyrocketing crime rate, a fictional show depicting Black people selling drugs and murdering one another hit too close to home. "I don't need to see *The Wire* for all that," she told me, "I can watch the news."

I recently found an email exchange with a journalist friend about *The Wire*, and his take was more critical. To him, Simon and the cadre of celebrated White crime novelists he tapped for his writers' room—George Pelecanos, Dennis Lehane, and Richard Price—"milked the hell outta the Negro pathology vein" while blithely inserting "nigger" into the dialogue every step of the way.

"We both know that things are playing out in our community that hardly need to be sugarcoated," he wrote, "but we also appreciate that Black Baltimore is tremendously complex and multifaceted." And its history informs that.

Sometimes there were glimpses of Baltimore's past. In a third-season episode titled "Middle Ground," a woman contrasts the crime and police violence in her neighborhood to a time from her youth when residents felt safe and a friendly beat cop knew just about everyone's name. In the same episode, Major "Bunny" Colvin tours parts of West Baltimore with Councilman Tommy Carcetti and points out a building that used to house a White-owned funeral home. According to Colvin, the owner once declared that he would service Black people only if he could "bury them all at once."

Before Proposition Joe is executed, he points to his grandparents' beautiful wedding photo and reminds his nephew Cheese that his grandfather was "the first colored man to own a home in Johnson Square," in East Baltimore. These scenes subtly convey societal shifts, but there's not much explanation about the circumstances that made the woman's neighborhood unsafe or inspired the funeral director's racist comment, or how Prop Joe's family went from breaking racial housing barriers to drug dealing two generations later.

"All the pieces matter," a phrase uttered by jaded Detective Lester Freamon in the first season of *The Wire*, became one of the show's catchphrases. Yet key pieces of Black Baltimore are missing. For instance, Baltimore, for all its industrialization, was once the largest segregated city south of the Mason-Dixon Line, and it still carries the residue of discrimination. I would have liked to have seen that acknowledged in *The Wire*. The program never touched on the fact that White flight after desegregation resulted in economic divestment, making the city vulnerable to increased crime. There is no mention of how so much of West Baltimore has never bounced back after the rioting that erupted in the wake of Martin Luther King's assassination destroyed it. Or how the shuttering of Bethlehem Steel, one of the largest companies in an industry that once employed generations of Black men, helped to buoy another—the illegal drug trade.

In 2019 I read an article in which Laura Lippman, a best-selling crime novelist and David Simon's wife, discussed her latest book, *Lady in the Lake*. From the title alone I figured that she was referencing the unsolved murder of Shirley Parker, a young Black woman whose body was found in the fountain of Druid Hill Park Reservoir in 1969. Lippman, who grew up in Baltimore, said she had never heard about Shirley Parker until 1990, when she was a reporter at the *Baltimore Sun*. "Of course, part of the reason I never heard about it was that it received very little coverage in the daily newspapers. I thought this was so interesting," she told the *Washington Post*. Of course you never heard of it, I thought, because you were a White girl in Baltimore during the 1960s and likely didn't encounter or know much about the city's Black residents. That's an example of the residue of segregation and discrimination I mentioned earlier.

Parker's murder was big news in the Black community. I was seven at the time, and I remember all of the adults I knew talking about it. The *Afro-American*, the city's Black newspaper, reported on it exhaustively, featuring pictures of the glamorous Parker, who was a secretary for the Urban League and a bookkeeper and barmaid at the Sphinx Club, a West Baltimore institution. For a while, on the anniversary of her murder the paper would recap the tragedy, noting that her killer was never found. Many of us old enough to remember never looked at the Druid Hill Park Reservoir fountain, with its delightful colored lights, the same way again.

These days I think a lot about the erasure of vibrant Black communities, either by violence like the Tulsa Race Massacre; so-called urban renewal like in the Black Bottom district of Detroit; gentrification like I've experienced living in Brooklyn; or the neglect that Black areas of Baltimore and other cities have endured for decades. I think about how sometimes our aspirational tendencies can prevent us from appreciating what we had because we are made to think it wasn't good enough. We must tell the stories about the places we inhabit—the good, the bad, and the mundane—lest they be forgotten.

In a 2012 post on his blog, *The Audacity of Despair: Collected prose, links and occasional venting from David Simon,* he writes:

> To be clear: I don't think *The Wire* has all the right answers... It may not even ask all the right questions. True, *The Wire* was fiction, and true, too, it was operating in the medium of American television, which is premised on entertainment above all. But concede at least that the problems depicted in *The Wire* are an actual dynamic in places like West Baltimore, where real people are marginalized or destroyed as a systemic function.

I can respect that, but I also know that West Baltimore was, and is, much more than that.

ষ্

JULIA CHANCE is a journalist and author whose work has appeared on Sisters From AARP, TheRoot.com, and Ebony. com and in magazines including *Essence*, *Ebony*, *Heart & Soul*, and Shop Smart. She is the author of *Sisterfriends: Portraits of Sisterly Love*, a photo-essay book celebrating the bonds of African American women who are sisters by blood or through close friendship. She remains a die-hard *Wire* fan.

6

Where da Hood At? The Heartbeat of Baltimore *The Wire* Didn't Detect

By Ericka Blount Danois

In 2002, I first learned about the upcoming HBO show *The Wire* from actor Andre Royo, who got the call that he got the part to play the character Bubbles while we were at the Sundance Film Festival in Utah. I was there covering the festival as a freelancer for *The Source* and supporting my friend Mums for his short *Morning Breath*. A few months later I took a staff writer job with the *Baltimore City Paper* and moved my family from Queens, New York.

I caught up with Andre in Baltimore about midway through the show's tapings for the first season. Andre was sleeping in the basement of a friend's house and spending time at drug rehabilitation centers, getting in character for Bubbles, who eventually became relegated to the basement of his sister's house because of his drug addiction. Andre helped me garner interviews with the actors and eventually with the writers and chief architects of *The Wire* for the *City Paper* and other local outlets, including *Baltimore* magazine and the *Baltimore Sun*.

I had grown up in 1980s Washington, DC, at the height of the crack era, when people would say DC stood for Dodge City because of the number of shootings. One year we had more murders than days of the year, as the murder total topped 436 by November 1990. We often had to escape shootings, running and hiding in bushes at parties and go-gos because of rival crews coming to fight.

I wasn't unfamiliar with the primary focus of *The Wire*—a show about a police task force assigned to topple a drug crew, and the larger theme about the gray areas between the good guys and the bad guys. Creator David Simon told me during an early interview, before the show premiered: "The economic machine, it will use everybody. If you're strong, it has a place for you; if you're weak, it has a place for you. All of its employees are brutally interchangeable—that is the theme."

I understood this. DC Mayor Marion Barry had created social programs and summer and year-round job programs for us starting at age fourteen, but it wasn't enough. The allure of ridiculous amounts of fast money was too great. There weren't many people we knew who were not touched by the drug epidemic—either selling small-time or using drugs or having family members or friends who did. These were regular, everyday people—many of them teenagers with retail jobs after school, some straight-A students, some middle-class, some sharing an efficiency apartment with many members of their families. They weren't all sinister or dysfunctional; more than that, they weren't all committed solely to the life.

When I interviewed Little Melvin Williams, the drug kingpin of Baltimore whom the character Stringer Bell is based on, he talked incessantly about the loves of his life, his wife of many decades and his two daughters, who were in college. After serving many years in prison, he expressed regrets about what his drug empire had done to Baltimore. Back in DC, my sister had attended a Christian camp with Rayful Edmond, whose reign in DC was comparable to Little Melvin's in Baltimore in the eighties. He was a devout Christian and, to hear tell from the camp members, a decent guy. People who were in the life weren't just one-dimensional characters. They were figuring out how to survive in a place that didn't offer many substantive options.

The extent of the efforts to show the complexity of fictional characters who mimicked people like Little Melvin or small-time drug dealers just trying to keep up with the Joneses or people trying to make extra cash on the side of their legitimate jobs was generally limited to turkey giveaways on Thanksgiving by fictional dealers on television and on film. Few films (*Paid in Full* was among the exceptions) treated dealers as people who dealt with the mundanity of life with equal time to the drama of the drug game. *The Wire* wasn't much different.

De'Londa Brice, Namond's mother on *The Wire*, who forced him to sell drugs, was unfamiliar to me. "What you mean Kenard took the stash?" she tells him in "That's Got His Own," episode twelve of Season 4. "Look at me, boy. Kenard got to feel some pain for what he did." I knew mothers who went outside and told their sons they couldn't be outside on the corners or who stepped to other dealers and told them not to allow their sons to participate. I didn't know any mothers who intentionally sentenced their kids to death or jail.

In DC, as a teenager, I watched police officers harass young Black boys who were sitting outside doing nothing other than talking and laughing. Later, as an adult, I learned about an entire Gun Trace Task Force in Baltimore that robbed civilians and drug dealers. I personally sat through a trial of six police officers indicted for the killing of Freddie Gray and watched them all get off while Gray's mother wailed in pain in the courtroom.

Largely crafted by White Baltimore City detective-turned-schoolteacher Ed Burns and White *Baltimore Sun* crime-reporter-turned-television-writer David Simon, assisted by a writers' room comprising other White male writers, *The Wire*, while showing the dysfunctional nature of Baltimore City police, particularly the hierarchy of the department, didn't show the kind of brutality and terror that happens (and happened) at the hands of police every day in the hood, especially before cellphone cameras came on.

But more than that, what I missed in the show is the mundanity of the everyday growing up in the hood. Every day wasn't do or die. We fell in love. Drug dealers got out of the game. They raised families and passed down money so their children could go to college and have better lives. They loved their wives. Teenagers took their girlfriends to the movies on the bus and got ice cream afterward. Rival crews warred for turf. And teenagers played Connect Four, did their homework, danced at the clubs, and talked trash.

When I worked at the *City Paper*, I interviewed residents at the McCulloh Homes low-rise housing projects as the television crew filmed and footballs wobbled through the air and children played basketball in the alleys.

"I don't like the fact that they do this here, but they won't go out to the upper-class neighborhoods and film late at night, even though the drugs are out there too," twenty-nine-year-old Sharron Dawkins said. "Overall, I'm upset because it will show this area as nothing but drugs and violence, and there's more to it than that."

Dawkins complained that film crews intruded on the neighborhood, making noise late at night and asking residents to accommodate them.

"They would come down and tell you that you were in the way and you had to move even if you were standing in front of your own house. They were knocking on people's doors late at night and telling them they couldn't make noise or walk certain places. They even told people they couldn't dry their clothes on the clothesline, to take their clothes down because they were filming."

While some residents didn't appreciate the production and its portrayal of their neighborhood, others were more accepting.

"Some aspects of what they were filming might be credible in that drugs and violence are going to happen," twenty-nine-year-old McCulloh Homes resident Joel Johnson said, holding his one-year-old son in his arms as he walked down Druid Hill Avenue. Still, he noted, "It ain't where you at, it's how you're living. It's not as bad as it used to be, but the drug population is not just here. It's everywhere."

After I rewatched the series nearly two decades after it aired, and after nearly two decades of living in Baltimore, it's easy for me to see the draw for fans. The dialogue is authentically Baltimore— quirky, hood, and witty. The characters are fascinating, smart, and entertaining. David Simon and Ed Burns constructed the largest cast of principal Black characters in television history, in a diversity of roles. We end up rooting for an openly gay stickup kid named Omar, played expertly by Michael K. Williams, who robs drug dealers and saunters in broad daylight with a sawed-off shotgun, with his oil duster floating behind him. He has a moral code: no bystanders or taxpayers get caught up in the mix and no killing on Sundays. He doesn't kowtow to a boss and he's loyal to his lovers. There's never been a Black character like him on any other television show.

Andre Royo's character, Bubbles, is a sympathetic and smart low-bottom heroin addict, born from a real-life police informant by the same name who died from AIDS.

Stringer Bell, played with swagger by Idris Elba, epitomized the sexiness of the hood bop walk and had the itch to make it and be accepted by the mainstream for his formidable business brains.

Then there's a gang of classic one-liners from the show. One of the most memorable, or iconic even, comes from Baltimore's own Felicia Pearson, who played Snoop. "How my hair look?" she asks Michael Lee, played by Tristan Wilds, just before he shoots her. Plus there are several laugh-out-loud dark-humor moments nudged in between all the dysfunction.

Felicia Pearson (Snoop) doesn't worry about her hair in this shot with a hat on.
Photo courtesy of HBO

But there's something quiet that's missing from *The Wire* and the show's intoxicating characters.

Prop Joe, played by Robert F. Chew, is the pleasant-faced ruler of the drug game on the East Side of Baltimore. In real life, Chew taught my kids piano at the Arena Playhouse, an African American theater that has trained actors for decades, including Howard Rollins. Chew also toured with some of the top musicals around the country.

In real life, Anwan Glover, who played Slim Charles, lived a few blocks from me in Washington, DC, and founded the Peaceoholics there to help young people and to help stem the murder rate after three of his brothers were gunned down.

Sonja Sohn, who played detective Kima, is a well-known poet who performed in legendary venues like the Nuyorican Poets Cafe alongside Saul Williams, Willie Perdomo, and jessica Care moore.

In real life, Black people in the game have ambitions outside of the game, have hobbies, love interests, and functional family relationships. With *The Wire*, you get the sense that the writers have a fascination for the Black characters, particularly the ones in the hood, but not a love for them. There's no sense that people who have grown up in the hood are leaders—that they've created community and survived as a result despite everything against them. That they have normal angst and identity crises and internal lives that have nothing to do with outside forces bringing them down.

Meanwhile, White characters like McNulty, played by Dominic West, are able to grow emotionally and have a loving relationship with a girlfriend toward the end of the series. Poor White characters in the game in the second season have family scenes on the playground doing normal, mundane things.

The Black characters are denied fulfilling lives or even just a boring day.

And somehow, although the intent, according to Simon and Burns, was to give equal time to the police and the drug dealers, the police officers still come out as the heroes to root for. In real life, Baltimore police officers were investigated by the Department of Justice, which issued a scathing report, citing incidents like a police officer slapping an innocent woman for accidentally bumping into him, police urinating and defecating on Black suspects' beds and clothes during raids, and police strip-searching a woman on the sidewalk in broad daylight after a routine stop for a busted taillight. Dozens of cops from Baltimore's Gun Trace Task Force went to jail.

The Wire is masterfully constructed television and storytelling with a riveting narrative about the decay of our cities, how no one will escape the fallout of racism, and the murderous failings of capitalism. It tells bleak stories with compassion. If only it told the joy of the mundane of the Black folks living through it all with equal compassion, it would be television perfection.

ъа

ERICKA BLOUNT DANOIS has worked as a writer, author, researcher, and producer for a number of projects, including the book *Love, Peace and Soul*, which detailed the history of the show *Soul Train* and its host; the documentaries *Time Is Illmatic and Tupac (Untitled)*; and the PBS series *Finding Your Roots*. As a journalist she has worked as a writer, editor, and producer for the *New York Times*, the *Washington Post*, the *Wall Street Journal*, *ESPN the Magazine*, *People*, *Playboy*, and MTV, among others.

Bunk (Wendell Pierce) and Lester (Clarke Peters) know that all the pieces that matter.
Photo courtesy of HBO

PART 3
All Systems Down

Introductory Overview

By Ronda Racha Penrice

One of the sad realities too many Americans just realized in the aftermath of George Floyd's murder by Minneapolis police officer Derek Chauvin back in 2020 is that American institutions don't serve us all. In 2002, when *The Wire* premiered, that truth was even less well-known. Its roots run deep but originate in one place: racism. Back in 2019, David Simon himself noted on Twitter that "the flight of the white tax base en masse from West Baltimore dates back to 1955 to 1957. No slums in those neighborhoods just frightened whites fearing the blockbust and running with all the tax money over the county line. They didn't flee slums. They ran with the $$$."

That trend had begun even earlier than the 1950s. In 1901, as shared in *The Nation*'s 2019 story "Who Broke Baltimore? We Did," White residents in West Baltimore protested converting a half-empty German-language school into a high school to serve the neighborhood's Black students. At the time, the *Baltimore Sun* justified their protests by asserting that it is a "self-evident fact that the presence of a negro school, or of any negro institution whatever in a neighborhood where hite people reside, will lower the value of their property and that the presence of such a school will be an incentive for negroes to move into the neighborhood and by so doing further lower the value of property and reduce the taxable basis of the city."

What do the actions of the 1950s and 1900s have to do with now or the real Baltimore of the fictional *The Wire*? Plenty. For decades, city and federal policies in Baltimore worked to contain its Black population. Not even manicured lawns kept the government from proposing a highway in the middle of the Black Rosemont community in West Baltimore. While that one didn't succeed, other policies destroying the infrastructure of Baltimore's Black community did. If a city doesn't want certain people to live there, why on earth would it provide them services to remain there?

Baltimore's critics point to the city's Black leadership as the source of failure, ignoring the long history of exclusion that preceded Kurt Schmoke's 1987 election as the city's first Black mayor and the elections of subsequent Black mayors. Freddie Gray's death in police custody in 2015 represented many. It was more than just one. Despite nationally publicized protests, no officers were held accountable. That those police officers were also Black matters little. The essays found here in "All Systems Down," whether it's Mekeisha Madden Toby breaking down Laetitia and Chiquan's violent encounter at school in Season 4, the "education" season, or Adom M. Cooper exploring the connections between *The Wire* and the January 6 Capitol riot at the top of 2021, leave no doubt that there is no urgency in any institution when it comes to serving Black people in Baltimore and beyond.

7

The Wire's Hard Truths About How Our
Schools Fail Us All

By Mekeisha Madden Toby

Whenever the issue of social and financial parity between Black and White Americans is raised, that discourse is incomplete without discussing the disparity within the educational system. The fact is schools in urban America, attended mostly by marginalized Black and Brown people, are underfunded, crowded, and sometimes violent, with Black students, according to the United Negro College, 3.8 times more likely to receive an out-of-school suspension. And without oversimplifying things, bad schools lead to undereducated kids who turn to crime when the system fails them. And this is what ultimately happened to Michael (Tristan Wilds), Namond (Julito McCullum), Randy (Maestro Harrell), and Duquan (Jermaine Crawford) in Season 4 of *The Wire*. So credit must be given to the drama's chief architects, David Simon and Ed Burns, and their writers for daring to unpack those inequities way back in 2006 and show the school-to-prison pipeline long before it was fashionable to do so or even had a recognizable name.

Perhaps this is one of the reasons why "Home Rooms," episode three, stands out in our collective memories. The installment focuses on former Baltimore Detective Roland "Prez" Pryzbylewski (Jim True-Frost), who, after accidentally shooting a plainclothes officer, quits the force and becomes an eighth-grade teacher. It is in Prez's class, where Michael, Namond, Randy, and Duquan are students, that viewers watch a bullying situation escalate and turn really terrible rather quickly. One of the boys' classmates, Chiquan (Tiffani Holland), an attention-loving girl with a penchant for trash talk, decides to focus her ire on a girl of lesser means named Laetitia (Charmaine McPhee). Chiquan antagonizes her by flashing a bright light from her wristwatch in Laetitia's face. A fight breaks out soon after, but Prez breaks it up.

Growing increasingly angry for being picked on by Chiquan, Laetitia decides to exact her own brand of justice and revenge later by bringing a boxcutter to class. This time Chiquan does little more than make a face at Laetitia, but this is all the excuse she needs, and when Prez turns his back to write on the chalkboard, Laetitia jumps up to confront Chiquan, who also jumps up, in reaction. Chiquan is unafraid, but perhaps she should be, because Laetitia quickly cuts Chiquan down to size by slashing her cheek with her boxcutter. Chiquan falls to the floor in pain as blood gushes from her face. Prez, who is frozen in horror, attempts to disarm Laetitia, but she swings her arm and threatens to slice him up next.

The whole class stands back behind Prez, nonplussed that Laetitia and Chiquan's row has escalated to blood and violence. But English teacher Grace Sampson (Dravon James) is unfazed as she, in one fell swoop, cuts through the crowd and slaps Laetitia to disarm her. Ms. Sampson then tells another student to call 911 and get the nurse and tells Chiquan to hold on to her face to slow the flow of blood. Clearly, this is not Ms. Sampson's first de-escalation, and even if Prez is paralyzed with uncertainty, she knows she can't be. The other students are counting on her to be a coolheaded adult, and so she is and tells them to go and sit down in their seats.

It is also worth noting how Duquan, Michael, Randy, and Namond react. Duquan goes to Laetitia's side and turns on a battery-operated fan to cool her off. He had found and fixed the miniature fan, and now he seems to know its purpose—to cool off a hotheaded classmate in shock. PTSD sufferers recognize each other so easily. Which makes you wonder how much senseless bloodshed and violence this boy had seen in his life. Then there is Michael, who never gets up from his desk. He just sits there and quizzically watches the scene unfold as if he's a detached spectator watching a television series. Meanwhile, Namond and Randy stand behind Prez in shock and confusion.

And just like that, in under two minutes, Burns, Simon, and company (the teleplay is credited to Richard Price, from a story by Price and Burns) take a random and irrational act of violence and turn it into a mirror that forces us all to examine not only ourselves, but also the systemic racism and classism that allow things like this to happen. As a Black viewer, you question who you are in this fray. Are you Laetitia or Michael? Are you Randy and Namond or Duquan? Or perhaps you are Grace Sampson. Do you help or hurt? Do you watch and do nothing or try to help the victimizer, who is also a victim? If

Michael (Tristan Wilds) is unmoved by an act of violence in the classroom in Season 4 of *The Wire*. Photo courtesy of HBO

you are White, are you Prez, unable to take action because you don't understand? Or will you try to help those whom you can help another time and another day?

Perhaps a breakdown will help. Let's start with Laetitia. No, she didn't have to bring a boxcutter to class to solve her problem with Chiquan. But clearly Laetitia had been picked on before, and for whatever reason, she decided violence was the only answer. By choosing violence, this poor Black girl chose criminalization. She will be labeled as such and forced to survive in institutions, where she will repeat this same action or have it repeated on her. Heck, given Laetitia's choice of "solutions," chances are she had already started down that path and was already in the system. She, of everyone involved, was failed most by the system, because Laetitia didn't have anywhere to go when the bullying became too much.

Then there is Chiquan. Disfigured for life, she has also been failed by the system. While it may be hard to sympathize with bullies, nothing she did or said warranted a slice to the face. Did she start the fight in the first place? Yes, but perhaps if she'd had better guidance and some way to channel her snark into something positive, she would've known better than to mess with an already wounded Laetitia. In a better funded school, it's nice to think, Chiquan would've been in the drama club or perhaps on the pep squad.

What about Prez? This man is just trying to teach math. He clearly wasn't taught the proper way to handle fights, or he'd known that simply "breaking" up the first altercation wasn't going to be enough. There should have been a system in place under which he could have sent these two girls somewhere so that they could talk and hash things out in a nonviolent way. Prez also needed better support and proper de-escalation training. Grace Sampson knew how to intervene when things got bloody, but one could argue that even she wasn't equipped to prevent these types of brutal occurrences from happening.

But, in the end, it comes back to Michael, Namond, Randy, and Duquan. With the exception of Duquan, who actually tried to help Laetitia, all of them were spectators. Fans of *The Wire* later learn that Duquan, whose family struggled with poverty and homelessness, falls victim to drug abuse and eventually becomes a heroin addict, by the end of Season 5. Randy, who attempted to help the police later in Season 4, loses his loving foster mother and the protection and comfort of her home after drug dealers retaliate and firebomb her house to punish Randy for snitching. By the end of Season 5, fans learn that Randy is no longer the sweet and precocious kid who sold candy and passed out political fliers. The system failed and hardened him, and Sergeant Ellis Carver (Seth Gilliam), who turned him into an informant, failed him most of all, by not protecting him and keeping his word.

Despite showing Prez an aptitude for math, Michael eventually turns to the streets. At first he works for Marlo (Jamie Hector) and his crew to repay them for killing his stepfather, who sexually abused him, until he starts to see flaws within their organization. Marlo and his crew think Michael is snitching to the cops, which he's not, and so Snoop (Felicia Pearson) tries to kill Michael, but he shoots and kills her first. Now Michael is a cold-blooded killer picking up where Omar (Michael K. Williams) left off and robbing drug dealers. In fact, the only one among the four to make it out is Namond. Fate had better a design for the son of Wee-Bey (Hassan Johnson), who ultimately let retired cop "Bunny" Colvin (Robert Wisdom) and his wife adopt Namond so that he could have a better life and not sell drugs.

Statistically speaking, it makes sense that only one of the four would beat the system. So, who are you in this scenario? Are you the one who made it out? And if you did, what can you do to help improve this stacked deck known as the educational system in America that's against so many? If you are the Namond in your world but grown and with kids, you have to figure out a way to stop your Black children from becoming statistics as well. If you are Prez or Grace, you have to find kids you can save from the system even if you can't save them all. And if you are Randy, Michael, Laetitia, Chiquan, or Duquan, for that matter, you must believe there is still hope, even when the system seems designed to throw you away.

❧

MEKEISHA MADDEN TOBY is a Los Angeles-based journalist who fell in love with books and words as the second-eldest daughter of an English teacher. The Detroit native, wife, and mother has covered television and other aspects of the entertainment industry for over twenty years. In addition to serving as a staff editor for TVLine.com, she has written for outlets such as *TV Guide*, Shondaland.com, *Essence*, the *Detroit News*, the *Los Angeles Times*, *People*, Mom. me, and *espnW*. She also has her own podcast, *TV Madness with Mekeisha Madden Toby.*

8

We Have to Save Us

By Danian Darrell Jerry

Surviving the hood in America is hard. Like superhard. I hate to say it, but the saying "shit rolls downhill" is real. On a literal and metaphysical level. The city officials and the police officers in *The Wire* look like the same city officials and police officers in my city, Memphis. In every city. In your city, the mayor and the city council and the board of education play a sad game. Nobody gets a throne. Nothing gets accomplished. People with money live in certain parts of your city, and people who are poor live in the worst parts of your city.

Being Black in America, we feel unprotected. Exposed to a world that can snatch you anytime, anyplace. Being Black in America, I feel uncertain. I worry at every moment. Not on the outside, though. It's the kind of worry that Omar puts in the back of your mind 'cause he shot your friend and let you go. The hood might snatch your best friend and your cousin and your sister and let you live to tell the tale. And then you have to go get a job like Poot at Foot Locker and think about them for the rest of your life.

Black people need each other. We can't make it without each other. We don't sell dope by ourselves. We join gangs and crews. We work for Avon, Marlo, Proposition Joe, whoever got that work. Even Black folks who don't like crowds need a chosen few or at least a listening ear like Butchie, somebody to talk and vent with. The world is tough on Black people, so we hold each other's hands so we can survive. We do this without even realizing it most of the time. Proposition Joe had Cheese. Marlo had Chris and Snoop. Avon and Stringer couldn't function without each other, even though the two of them eventually forgot that.

But the groups fail too. On *The Wire*, the crews failed the corner boys. Dozens of desperate Black teenagers looked to Stringer and Avon for guidance and leadership. Avon sacrificed the Black people who worked for him like they were garbage. All for his corners. Stringer Bell lies to everybody close to him. D'Angelo dies trying to be strong for his family. Wallace thought he was following his friends when Bodie and Poot led him to the room where they killed him. Wallace cried and begged, but it didn't matter, because if Bodie and Poot let the boy live they knew they would die with him. Nobody was ever safe on *The Wire*, and the bonds they formed saved them only a little while.

On *The Wire*, there is no safe place for Black people. Not in the hood, the courthouse, school, work. We can search every row house, every street corner. Follow the rules. Keep it real. Be true to the game. In the end, you gotta face danger. The hood consumes without warning or discrimination. It creeps up on you when your back is turned, like Kenard did Omar. If you live in the hood, just expect anything to happen at any given time, because it can.

Poor Black people are always waiting for the ball to drop. Somebody got laid off. Somebody OD'd. Somebody lost another loved one. We cope with the danger and the uncertainty in different ways. Some of us self-medicate, like Bubbles and Dukie. Some sell drugs, like Avon, Stringer, and Proposition Joe. Others go buck wild and start robbing everybody, like Omar and Michael. Some even try to change the hood for the better, like "Cutty" Wise and "Bunny" Colvin.

Everybody on *The Wire* is trapped in a constant state of fear and discomfort. Even the kids feel the tension. Most of them are forced into the drug game as soon as they're old enough to count. Most poor people never escape places like Franklin Terrace towers, and this fear turns us against each other. Or just puts us in constant survival mode. Or both.

In Season 4, Marlo walks into a convenience store and grabs a bottle of water and two lollipops as a frustrated security guard watches in disbelief. Like, *look at this nigga*! Marlo stares straight through the security guard and strolls out the store without a care in his fucked-up world. Outside the convenience store, the rent-a-cop makes a huge mistake. He actually confronts Marlo and tries to express frustration and helplessness to the heartless sociopath.

"I'm a man," the security guard says as he steps in front of Marlo, silently screaming inside. He even puts his finger in Marlo's face. "And you just clipped that shit like you don't even know I'm there."

He should have stayed in the store and let Marlo go about his business, but he forgets to stay out the way. The Asian lady working the cash register knows what's up and doesn't say anything. Instead, she lets Marlo walk out the store with whatever he wants. She's not from the hood, but even she knows the unspoken rule to "stay out of Marlo's way."

I've been that cashier in a convenience store, and I never chased anybody for any reason. One dude ran out of the store with a whole case of Corona. The beer wasn't mine, and it wasn't worth the trouble. Or my life.

When the security guard gets off work, he bumps into Chris and Snoop. And everybody knows what it means when Chris and Snoop post up. *How will his kids eat now?* is all I could think.

*

In Season 3, Major Howard Colvin, Bunny to his family and close friends, drives an unmarked car through West Baltimore and sees everything from wild-haired addicts limping through the streets to a corner boy who actually tries to sell him, a cop, a police major, a bag of heroin.

The major's only a few months from retirement, but he wants to

Major Colvin (Robert Wisdom) creates "Hamsterdam," which becomes the main plot point in Season 3 of *The Wire*. Photo courtesy of HBO

help his community as much as he can before he leaves the force. He knows the beast he works for, and he knows the neighborhoods where he grew up are going to hell. The cops who break fingers and call the Black boys "shit birds" technically work under him. He knows Clay Davis and Mayor Royce, and he's seen a thousand McNultys crying over dead Black people.

Colvin knows the problems in West Baltimore are too big, so he tries to confine the drugs to one area, a free zone where groups can sell, buy, and use dope like it's legal. Trying to give poor Black people a safe place to live, he loses his pension and all he's worked for. The police department fails Major Colvin and the Black folks in West Baltimore just like the police in America have failed us.

Colvin knows the bonds and the blood mean nothing when the environment forces the people to kill each other just to make it. Namond's mother, De'Londa, would send him to the corner until he got shot or sent to jail for the rest of his life like his daddy, Wee-Bey. Colvin spent most of his life protecting the community, but in the end learns that the people have to protect and serve each other. His hope is Namond will pull other Black people to success.

In that same season, Dennis "Cutty" Wise got the same idea.

After Cutty makes parole, he returns to the only life he has ever known—the same drug trade that sent him to prison. Cutty finds work muscling corners for Avon Barksdale. But the name he earned in West Baltimore and Jessup Correctional Institution means nothing in the fickle currency of street credibility. Young pups working the corners don't give a damn about the good old days. The bad new days belong to them. After several failed returns to the game, Cutty follows his heavy conscience and leaves the hustler life in his rear view.

"It ain't in me no more," he says, with conviction in his trembling voice, as he bares his truth to the drug bosses and to himself.

Cutty trades in his street credibility, his onetime fame or infamy, depending on which side of the street coin you fall, for his government name, Dennis, and a boxing gym to lure kids off the streets. His heightened sense of purpose and renewed ties to West Baltimore yield results, with his protégés including even the Spider Bags boy who offered drugs to Colvin.

*

Malik "Poot" Carr doesn't adopt anybody or open a gym, but he does offer the conventional way out. During the show's five-season run, Poot, who begins *The Wire* as a low-level drug dealer working with his best friend, Preston "Bodie" Broadus, murders an unsuspecting associate, serves a prison sentence, and endures a beating under the baseball bats of a rival drug crew. These events lead Poot to the night he runs for his life. Bodie isn't as fortunate; shadowy gunmen execute him over suspicion of snitching to the police.

By *The Wire*'s series finale, Poot quits the corners to work in a shoe store. When Duquan "Dukie" Weems creeps into the store looking for a job, Poot offers as much helpful advice as he can. Each recognizes the other's face, and they communicate without using names. Outside the corners wait, and the corners know their names. Hesitant to push the storefront door, Dukie returns to the corners and the drug trade. Poot shakes his head and laughs at himself, thankful to have been saved. But the city officials didn't save him or any of his friends. Neither did the police and neither did the schools. He's still Black and unprotected in America. Just a smidge safer than before and hopeful about the future. Maybe he can make the world a little bit safer for somebody else.

ક

Danian Darrell Jerry is a writer, teacher, and hip-hop musician with a master of fine arts in creative writing from the University of Memphis. He is a Voices of Our Nations Arts Foundation (VONA) fellow, a fiction editor at *Obsidian: Literature and Arts in the African Diaspora*, and founder of Neighborhood Heroes, a youth arts program that employs comic books and literary arts. Publications or anthologies in which his work appears include *Fireside Fiction*, *Black Panther Tales of Wakanda*, the *Magazine of Fantasy and Science Fiction*, and *Trouble the Waters: Tales from the Deep Blue*. He has also revised his first novel, *Boy with the Golden Arm*.

9

Girls in the Hood: Black Women
and *The Wire*

By Ronda Racha Penrice

Kima and Snoop are among *The Wire*'s most memorable characters. So much so that they often obscure *The Wire*'s notable missteps in representing Black women. Yes, both Nerese Campbell and Marla Daniels are presented as savvy and smart women who can more than hold their own in the rough-and-tumble world of politics. And Grace Sampson is an urban success story, escaping the streets to become an educator who is firm, highly capable, and loving. These women represent a small percentage, however. As a group, Black women, especially mothers, don't fare well on *The Wire*.

Namond's mom, De'Londa, appears more invested in her son selling drugs to keep her in the lifestyle to which she is accustomed than in Namond getting an education so that he can go a different route than his father, Wee-Bey, who ends up doing life in prison. In the first season, when Wallace goes "missing" before his death is confirmed, his mom, Darcia, is so high and so repulsive as a mother that she can't even be bothered by his whereabouts. Raylene, Michael's mother, is so much of an addict that she sells the last box of Rice-A-Roni, the only food in the house, leaving nothing for her youngest son, Bug, to eat.

And then there's Brianna, Avon Barksdale's sister and D'Angelo's mother. She keeps the money straight, plus Avon listens to her. Avon has so much respect for her that he puts her son, his nephew, in the game. Although there are early signs that he isn't built for the game the way his uncle is, his mother keeps forcing the game on him, and he ends up in prison. When it looks like he might turn on the organization, it's his mom who stresses how important it is for him to stay loyal. Still, he ends up dead in an apparent suicide. Detective Jimmy McNulty, who has been gunning for Stringer Bell and Avon, believes D'Angelo's death was a hit instead and mentions it to Donette, the mother of D'Angelo's son, who passes it along to Brianna. Later, when Brianna asks McNulty why he went to Donette, the mother of D'Angelo's son, her grandson, with his concerns and not her, he responds harshly, "Honestly, I was looking for somebody who cared about the kid."

These portraits fall in line with news stories of the Black-single-mother epidemic, a narrative dating back to the infamous Moynihan Report, as it's more popularly known, or *The Negro Family, The Case for National Action*, as it's officially titled, from 1965. That report unleashed the vicious stereotype of the Black single mother as a "welfare queen" sucking the life out of public institutions and society at large. With Black men being incarcerated and killed at alarming rates as the drug wars raged in the 1980s and 1990s, single-mother households became convenient scapegoats. And so it should be no surprise that *The Wire* unconsciously perpetuates some of these myths. That's not to say single-mother households on the brink don't exist or that women who make these disastrous choices are not real. Sadly, they are very real. The issue is the show's failure to provide the same context for many of the women characters that is provided for the men who are no saints themselves. Wee-Bey makes the right decision to let "Bunny" Colvin and his wife, Lolita, take in Namond, and all of the sudden he's father of the year?

If Avon is the way he is because his father was a heavyweight in the game, then wouldn't Brianna be too? Of course, astute fans of *The*

Wire know this. But the writers could have been a bit more explicit instead of just leaving it up for interpretation. Isn't how Brianna raised D'Angelo in line with how Avon was raised? Based on Brianna's experiences with the men in her life, was she completely wrong to assume her son would be unable to handle the weight? Were her visions of how a man handles himself not shaped by her father or the men she saw around her? How is it that she takes all the heat when she is far from the only one to blame? Also, how do structural racism and persistent socioeconomic failures not also impact Black women? Was Brianna not shaped by the same streets as Avon, Stringer, and Wee-Bey? Does she not have a business mind in line with Stringer's? Has she not also been cut off from the same opportunities beyond the drug game?

What happened in De'Londa's life to make her so dependent on men? Did our nation's Jim Crow educational system somehow spare her? Was there absolutely no redemption for a Darcia or a Raylene? Could they not struggle to get clean like Bubbles? Black mothers consistently fail their kids on *The Wire*, with no real attempts to explain why. And when Randy's foster mother, Anna Jeffries, tries to do right, the streets overcome her. Yes, we know the intent of *The Wire*'s architect, David Simon, was to show mass institutional failure on various fronts, but it just seems that either he and his writers didn't know or just forgot that Black girls and women live hood lives too.

That failure also shows up in *The Wire*'s portrait of young Black women as the men of the show routinely use and discard them. At a party, Wee-Bey takes Keisha, a dancer at Orlando's, the strip club that is Avon's front, into a bedroom to have sex despite it being more than clear that she is absolutely in no condition to consent to sex. The next morning, it's D'Angelo, not Wee-Bey, who realizes she is even dead. A young woman's life has ended, and her body is wrapped in a rug and left in a dumpster.

When Shardene, who only recently began seeing D'Angelo, brings up Keisha being missing, he brushes it off and instead steers the conversation to himself, voicing out loud that he isn't sure the drug game is for him. As Shardene commiserates, sharing that dancing isn't

Shardene (Wendy Grantham) and D'Angelo (Larry Gilliard Jr.)—the happy couple? Photo courtesy of HBO

exactly in her either and that there's no longevity in it because "I can't stay pretty forever," D'Angelo doesn't listen. Instead, he turns that moment into a sexual opportunity, disregarding both Keisha and Shardene.

Avon enlists the young and attractive Devonne to set Marlo up, but Marlo, through his soldier Chris Partlow, figures out Avon's play. In the moment, Chris and crew roll up on Avon's SUV, shooting it up, killing Tater, and injuring Avon. Marlo later catches up with Devonne and brutally kills her in front of her house by shooting her in each breast and her mouth. No lights come on in the house. Just like Keisha, Devonne is easily used and discarded.

The same goes for Tosha, the young woman in Omar's crew whom Omar's lover Dante accidentally shoots and kills during a heist gone wrong. Naturally, Kimmy, her partner in love and crime, is distraught by her death. Although Omar is also saddened by Tosha's death, and seems to feel guilty for pushing yet another Barksdale Organization robbery to make them pay for brutally murdering his lover Brandon, he still expects Kimmy to continue working with Dante, who frankly isn't that apologetic about his fatal mistake. As sincere as Omar's grief is, it's hard to fathom a man being asked to tolerate the same.

Many have praised *The Wire* for allowing viewers to see Black male deaths as far more meaningful than those of faceless thug-number-ones or -twos, but Black female deaths rarely occupy the same space. Who was Devonne, for instance? We know Avon hired her to seduce Marlo and set him up, but who *was* she? What was her motivation? Same goes for Keisha. Why was she dancing at Orlando's? What pushed her to become a stripper? How did Tosha and Kimmy even meet and fall in love? If it were another show, the argument could be made that these are minor characters not worthy of backstories. But that is the very thing that made *The Wire* different. It just didn't extend enough to its Black women characters.

All is not bleak, of course. As aforementioned, Kima and Snoop are *Wire* legends and groundbreaking portraits of Black lesbians for television. While some can argue that Kima Greggs was written as a man with a ponytail, her impact is undeniable. Showtime's *The L Word*, with Jennifer Beals as a star, debuted in 2004, two years after *The Wire*. So again, Kima is a trailblazing character who provided representation to a group that had historically never seen themselves presented with such complexity on the small screen.

As a cop, a partner, and later a parent, Kima has a full life and complications that lesbians on television did not have then. Immediately, the show establishes Kima as a lesbian, with no gray area. Kima counters pop culture depictions that lesbians exist solely to fulfill men's "girl-on-girl" action fantasies, a trope even found in the show itself. The most glaring example may be when Stringer rewards Avon with a threesome upon his return from prison. By contrast, Kima makes it clear that she loves women only and needs no man to "straighten" her out.

She isn't a so-called model minority, either. Kima has her flaws, especially in relationships, even if a lot of them fall under familiar male stereotypes, such as an inability to remain faithful. One of the reasons her ups and downs with her partner, Cheryl, still resonate so widely is because their issues are universal to a lot of couples. Sonja Sohn's portrayal of Kima, along with that of Melanie Nicholls-King as Cheryl, helped humanize Black queer women on television specifically and lesbians overall. That humanization, however, is one that Simon has admitted he can't take credit for.

During a cast reunion for *The Wire* at PaleyFest New York in 2014, reported by Time.com, Simon revealed that he had intended to kill Kima off after she was shot in the first season, but HBO exec Carolyn Strauss saved her. Simon has also admitted his limitations in writing women characters in general and has given credit to Sohn for bringing more to Kima than he put on the page. In a 2008 piece titled "Women and 'The Wire,'" *PopMatters* cited a conversation Simon had at Mystery One Bookstore (identified as *Mystery One* magazine by *PopMatters*) in Milwaukee in which he admitted that "I tend to suspect that my female characters are, to quote a famous criticism of Hemingway, men with tits." Regarding Kima, he shared, "Largely, I write her as a man and then, I confess, it's Sonja Sohn who adds all the subtlety in her performance."

Kima (Sonja Sohn) rescues a child in Season 5. Photo courtesy of HBO

For Snoop, the actual nickname for Felicia Pearson, the actress who played her, real-life experience made her most memorable. Pearson came on the show through Michael K. Williams, who spotted her in a Baltimore bar and brought her to *The Wire*. Born a crack baby, raised in foster care, and with a prison bid for murder on her record, Pearson, who was an active drug dealer when Williams met her, wasn't just a Baltimore native; she lived *The Wire*. And that authenticity seared through the screen. As one of Marlo's soldiers, she is just fierce. Unlike other Black women's deaths on the show, hers still means something. That's just how affecting it remains.

And, if we are being real, Snoop is the rare heroic portrayal of a poor Black woman. On another show, a murderer would not be heralded. But it's *The Wire*, and it's apropos for a show in which other murderers, like Avon, Stringer, Wee-Bey, and Slim Charles, not to mention Omar and more, toe that same line. But let's be honest, *The Wire* is as guilty of respectability politics as other shows. The difference is that in the context of this show, it is a progressive move when applied to a handful of Black women characters.

Kima, the show's undisputed Black woman star, is a cop, which is a respectable career and a background not often seen at this point in TV. Her partner, Cheryl, works in broadcast news. Grace Sampson is a teacher, a role that has historically been one of the backbones of the Black community but is still not as popular of a TV role for Black women as it should be. And Grace has the added distinction of rising from similar conditions as many of her students. This is communicated through her drug-addicted sister, Queenie (and Dravon James plays them both remarkably), in conversation with Cutty, Grace's old flame. It is also noteworthy that when Cutty comes calling, Grace doesn't falter. She is completely committed to looking forward and not going back, which is rarely depicted.

Then there is Marla Daniels, who progresses from the wife of Lieutenant Cedric Daniels to a city councilwoman, and Nerese Campbell, who has her eye on the mayoral throne. Because Black women, especially during the time of original airing, occupied those roles so rarely on TV, *The Wire*'s presentation of them, missteps and all, is, again, progressive. It is one of the rare bright spots of Black female representation on *The Wire*.

Ultimately *The Wire* is as guilty as all others in largely pathologizing and villainizing the Black woman and painting the ills that rock poor Black communities as almost solely a crisis of the Black male. In *The Wire*, Black men have a sense of agency Black women characters can't even think of obtaining. And that goes for both Kima and Snoop. As forceful as Nerese is, she never becomes as centralized a character as her actions perhaps warrant. And Marla's agency is presented as a thorn in her husband's spine, so much so that she is repaid by him becoming involved with a white woman. It's a subtle dig, but it is a dig nonetheless. On *The Wire*, ambitious Black women cannot have it all. And poor, struggling Black women don't even have a chance. It's not just a flaw; it's a tragedy.

10

Finding the Greater Truth: *The Wire* and Journalism

By Seve Chambers

As a Black journalist who found my way into the field just as *The Wire* began airing on HBO in 2002, I was drawn to the parts of the show that, to my eyes, offered scathing critiques of society's neglect of Black people. The show's final season put a spotlight on the dysfunctionality within journalism drawn from creator David Simon's many years of reporting on crime for the *Baltimore Sun*. It's a view consistent with all the other elements he examines in his city.

Interrogating American society through the lens of Baltimore in particular is a Simon trademark. But even with *The Wire*'s heightened awareness, especially around issues rarely raised regarding poverty and race, and obvious compassion, there are ways in which the series failed its Black cast, audience, and the community it set out to serve. Sadly, those failures mirror society at-large.

Theoretically, Simon, as a former journalist, should have understood how important responsible and accurate representation is for marginalized and underrepresented communities. Either Simon and his writers, mostly other White men, never felt a need to fully unpack this or their Whiteness stopped them. Consequently, there is a disconnect in *The Wire* between the journalism in the show and its Black citizens that, again, mirrors real life. Simon's fictional newsroom reenacted many of the large media controversies of the time. During this spotlight on the fourth estate, aka journalism, several cops, most notably McNulty, courtesy of his fabricated serial killer attacking the city's homeless population, leverage coverage from the paper to advance cases they are pursuing. The consequences of these actions play throughout the season, with some of the characters viewing this fabricated story as a golden opportunity and others frustrated with the erosion of journalistic ethics. Less spoken about, though, are the racial dynamics at work, with a mostly White journalism team covering a largely Black city. While this is true to life, the series also fails to critique the larger consequences of this condition and how the fourth estate tends to fail non-White people. The effects of this on the paper's reporting, and the stories that could be told, are hinted at within the show but are never fully explored. While one TV show cannot cover every issue, for *The Wire*, it was a missed opportunity to present more nuanced voices that could have greatly deepened the narrative.

At its core, the fifth season is the tale of an industry struggling to maintain its integrity. Through its take on the war on drugs and various aspects of the city's ecosystem, *The Wire* leans into gritty perceptions of Baltimore. The paper's coverage of the city constantly shifts to chasing buzzworthy stories. Space in the newspaper once reserved for minutes of City Hall meetings is now devoted to other story ideas. Reporters get reassigned to different sections—not on their beats or in their wheelhouse—and struggle to tell compelling stories, butting heads with their editors in the process. The fictional paper is seen as a rough reflection of its city, rifled with jadedness and bordering on loathing for the very metropolis it is tasked to cover. And who can blame these journalists for losing their faith when the paper is at the whim of rich executives who have little interest in informing the public? Rich executives who undermine that mission by slashing staff numbers when revenue projections are not immediately met?

The Wire strips away the glorified perception of the field with a portrayal of the *Baltimore Sun* as a place where hierarchies and personal ambitions are front and center. Newsroom politics are shown with considerable transparency as reporters and editors clamor for accolades and promotions. When a veteran cop whips up a series of falsified murders of homeless people, reporter Scott Templeton latches onto the story. In an obvious reference to real-life reporters who have been caught fabricating stories, his editors and fellow reporters start to notice the lack of evidence and inconsistencies in his reporting. Templeton's actions are supposed to have been inspired by a real *Sun* staffer whose story was retracted after several inaccuracies. David Simon has also shared that he drew from DC/Maryland/Virginia *New York Times* reporter Jayson Blair, who attended the University of Maryland. The rise of Blair into the ranks of the *New York Times* and his failure there fed into the erroneous perception of "affirmative action" hires as unqualified Black candidates especially, given jobs over presumably more qualified White candidates to meet diversity quotas. Critics pointed to the pressure to diversify newsrooms as the primary factor in Blair's swift and unwarranted ascent.

Like most newspapers, the *Times* has a subpar record of hiring Black journalists. But instead of the industry and its lack of inclusion being taken to task, it was Blair's pattern of plagiarism and his individual failure that echoed most loudly, which resulted in the penalizing of others. In the aftermath of the scandal, Gerald Boyd, the highest-ranking Black editor at the paper, and its White executive editor Howell Raines were forced to resign. But Black journalists not tied to Blair reported being treated as coconspirators in other newsrooms simply due to race. In the heat of the fallout, former *Washington Post* staffer and UC Berkeley Graduate School of Journalism professor Neil Henry penned the 2003 article "Racial Reverberations in Newsrooms After Jayson Blair" attesting to this for *Nieman Reports*, the publication of the Harvard-based Nieman Foundation for Journalism covering leadership in journalism.

Augustus "Gus" Haynes, played by Clark Johnson, who also directed *The Wire*'s first and last episodes, is always depicted as highly

Clark Johnson, who directed both the premiere and series finale, joined the cast in Season 5. Photo courtesy of HBO

capable. As one of the few Black editors shown on a consistent basis, he maintains order within the newsroom and makes sure everyone meets their deadlines. He is essentially relegated to being a voice of reason that calls out the unethical practices of his peers, which, based on my own experience in the newsroom, is not an uncommon role for Black journalists seeking to stand out and move up the ranks. Constant cuts to the newsroom and bureau closures at the paper push Gus to lament the changing landscape and the stories prioritized by his fellow editors. When an editor glosses over a scandal at a university accused of falsifying its diversity numbers, he even becomes visibly annoyed. Ultimately, he can do little about the paper's shift from covering the city with a wider scope of honesty to focusing on angles that have more award-winning potential. By the series's end, Gus's pushback against these changes results in his demotion. Although Gus is shown questioning the industry's overall direction from an ethical standpoint, he is also reflective of the uneasiness many Black journalists feel in raising their voices within largely White newsrooms.

Numerous accounts from current and former reporters support Gus's experiences. And, sadly, those Black voices who do rise to the status of editor are often in an even more uncomfortable position, further amplifying the marginalization and overall absence of Black voices in these spaces. On the heels of George Floyd's death, Black journalists became more vocal about the absence and marginalization. And we have the data to back it up.

According to statistics pulled from the American Society of News Editors and the Google News Initiative, in 2018 about 11 percent of the *Sun's* newsroom was Black. The percentage of Black people in positions of leadership was the same. White people constituted over 80 percent of the journalists in the newsroom and in key editorial positions. According to that same survey, 62 percent of the paper's readership was Black. The overall report, measuring diversity numbers in various newsrooms across the country, did not have comparable figures from 2001 to 2017, so it is impossible to see if there was a notable change from that time to 2018. In the wake of the summer of 2020, when racial discussions were occurring across many fields, journalism was not spared from this reckoning. Numerous journalists from publications coast to coast, including the *Washington Post*, shared stories of feeling disempowered and mistreated in their newsrooms, and the diversity imbalance at the *Baltimore Sun* was hardly anomalous when compared with other newspapers throughout the country. So it's no stretch to assume there were similar stories from Black journalists at the *Sun*, but it's probably even worse to work for a paper in a city whose population is two-thirds Black when that potential readership is ignored by the very paper built to cover it.

This, perhaps, explains the poor or nonexistent relationship the reporters on *The Wire* have with the local population. The series often explores the complexities of the city, and humanizes many aspects of it, as seen in the relationships cops like Kima and McNulty have within the community through their connections with characters like Bubbles and Bodie, but this dynamic seems inadequately fleshed out. It matters that there aren't enough Black reporters to connect with the local populace. Simon, who often drew upon his real-life experiences for *The Wire*, even mentioned in an interview with respected industry trade the *Columbia Journalism Review* how the majority of the reporters on the police beat, where many journalists cut their teeth, were White, noting that only one member of the four-man team he referenced was Black. In the same interview, he also mentions how White reporters viewed the beat and reporting on a city such as Baltimore as a badge of honor, which the show depicts. As real as it is, the sight of a largely Black city being covered by mostly White reporters feels jarring at best. Yet the show never addressed this in any substantive way. If one of *The Wire*'s main goals was to cover the stories of the rich and poor, haves and have-nots, powerful and powerless, how could race not figure more prominently here?

It's also notable that *The Wire* depicts only mainstream—read "White"—publications. The *Baltimore Afro-American*, one of the nation's oldest Black newspapers, founded in 1892, isn't referenced or seen in any form throughout the series. And neither is the *Baltimore Times*, a paper focused on non-crime-related stories about Baltimore's Black population since the 1980s. The reach of the Bramble family, who owns the *Times*, extends to neighboring areas in Maryland, such as Prince George County and Annapolis, where the family also publish area-specific editions. While a Black newspaper may not have typically covered crime as consistently as the *Sun*, ignoring the presence of Black media within a largely Black city seems like an oversight for a season focused on the daily role of journalism and media in a city's life cycle. Black publications frequently run columns on local issues, and surely would have written about community efforts to provide outlets for the Black youth in *The Wire*. For example, in the 1930s, the *Afro-American* launched its own initiative called "The Clean Block" aimed at addressing crime within the city and finding ways to improve the state of inner-city neighborhoods. Carl Murphy, former editor of the paper, also ran a column that addressed the lack of Black firefighters and politicians, as well as the need for a state-supported university for African Americans.

Surely a publication like the *Afro-American* would have featured Cutty, an ex-enforcer turned boxing-gym owner and the only consistent depiction of community efforts to combat crime, and his gym in a story. There's also a near absence of alternative newspapers or other publications native to the greater Baltimore area, publications that can delve into reporting that some of the major publications don't always have the resources to do. To exemplify this, Baltimore-based statewide newspaper the *Daily Record* appears briefly in *The Wire* as one such publication, beating the *Sun* to a transportation story after the *Sun* no longer has a reporter on that beat. This demonstrates not only how the existence of multiple newspapers benefits a community, but also how holding one news entity up as a holy grail, even as it is being criticized, is perhaps not the best idea. Different experiences need to be reflected, and no one news outlet can be tasked with telling every story. The same could be said of *The Wire*'s largely narrow focus on the *Sun*, especially when firing shots at the industry at-large. Yes, Simon knows the *Sun* best, but the potentially dangerous takeaway is that the *Sun*, provided it gets its act together, is the only newspaper that can amply serve Baltimore.

Even before journalism's decline became popular conversation, *The Wire* exposed its downward spiral, pointing to newsroom cuts and other adjustments hindering the industry's ability to serve the public good. The show demonstrated little faith in hardworking journalists' ability to guide the industry past award-hungry editors and board members prioritizing profits above all. And, sadly, *The Wire*'s observations have been proven right. The problem is the series did not go far enough. As we know today, the mainstream press erasure of, and blatant disregard for, Black people and our experiences is also a part of that crisis. Not sounding that alarm is a huge failure for *The Wire* that, frankly, exposes a worldview that is decidedly anti-Black regardless of how many Black actors populated the screen. The truth is *The Wire* succeeds despite some serious missteps. As the Black Lives Matter movement, which was particularly strong in Baltimore in the aftermath of Freddie Gray's death in police custody, has demonstrated, representation extends beyond cops, drug dealers, and city hall. And good journalism reflects that.

❧

SEVE CHAMBERS is a journalist based in Brooklyn. His words have appeared in the *Wall Street Journal*, *Fast Company*, the *Daily Beast*, *Vulture*, *Wax Poetics*, and other publications. He is currently working with former Gil Scott-Heron collaborator Brian Jackson on his memoir.

11

Bunk's Lesson About Giving a Fuck in *The Wire* and Real Life

By Adom M. Cooper

"There you go. Giving a fuck when it ain't your turn to give a fuck."
-Detective William "Bunk" Moreland talking to Detective James McNulty

This is one of my favorite quotes from *The Wire*, because it exposes how politicians, law enforcement, security, and intelligence officials conduct themselves based only on who is in front of them. In *The Wire*'s fictional universe, there is a clear dichotomy between the proactive and reactive actions these officials take.

Bunk's astute observation from the very first episode of *The Wire* proved apropos following the events of January 6, 2021, when a group of White supremacist insurrectionists stormed the US Capitol in an attempt to overturn the verified and fraud-free 2020 election. "We're going to the Capitol," President Trump tweeted prior. Parler, then tagged as the conservative Twitter or Facebook (or a combination of both, maybe mixed with Instagram), was full of right-wing folks directly talking about doing exactly what they did on January 6.

The "STOP THE STEAL!" and "TAKE OUR COUNTRY BACK" rhetoric was on full display and never hidden.

The US security apparatus created and implemented after 9/11 to stop foreign terrorism did not stop the country's own citizens, homegrown terrorists, from forcefully entering the center of our legislative branch of government. A Benghazi-style event happened at our seat of government, and the Capitol Police were told not to use their most aggressive tactics. Little to no proactive steps were taken to stop the insurrection from happening. The US National Guard was not called in right away, when it was time for law enforcement, security, and intelligence officials to proactively give a fuck. After the White supremacist insurrectionists forced their way into the Capitol building, killing Police Officer William "Billy" Evans, raiding the office of House Speaker Nancy Pelosi, and destroying federal property, they simply left and went home, like they had been party guests.

As a Black American male, I do not dare dream of openly talking about storming the US Capitol for ANY reason, showing up to do so, killing anyone—let alone Capitol Police officers—destroying federal property, walking out of the building, and living long enough to go home and sleep in my own bed. There are simple and overt actions Black folks do not dream of taking for fear of being executed on the spot. This reality is underscored throughout *The Wire*—primarily through establishing the wire on the Barksdale crew, the availability of resources to continue surveillance, and in how cities perceive their problems and threats versus reality.

At the start of the show, Baltimore PD are in hot pursuit of the Barksdale crew after D'Angelo Barksdale is acquitted for murder when a witness changes her story on the stand. Tremendous energy, time, and resources are spent to follow members of the crew and establish their movement and patterns, with the intent to bring them down. And the spark was one acquittal. One has to wonder: if D'Angelo had been convicted, what would Detective McNulty and his crew have done on the clock? They were concerned with the murders of Baltimore's Black citizens only in relation to procuring a respectable solved-murder rate. Today we talk about Black Lives Matter because the reality, as the show conveys, is that Black lives matter only as statistics, not as fellow breathing human beings.

A member of Lieutenant Cedric Daniels's crew on the police force, Roland "Prez" Pryzbylewski, figures out the code that the Barksdale crew is using. Countless man-hours are then spent on this. Where are the countless man-hours working on the history and conditions of Baltimore that created an environment conducive to the Barksdale crew even existing? The show also goes out of its way to rehabilitate the character of Prez (the only police officer in the entire show to fire his service weapon) as he goes from complete cop disaster saved by nepotism to respectable high school teacher. Again, the show does a great job of illustrating how systems and institutions save and protect folks of European descent and leave the rest of us to fend for ourselves.

Take the example of Detective McNulty's friend at the FBI. During one of his first visits to the FBI, McNulty sees how advanced and vast the surveillance techniques are. He watches a live video feed of a bust and is intrigued by how his local police unit could benefit. The FBI proactively gave a fuck about stopping drug dealers. But what if those resources were proactively used to go after folks who committed actions like on January 6? During a global pandemic, this group of individuals could have avoided the efficacy of facial recognition technology by heeding the Center for Disease Control's recommendation of mask wearing to prevent the spread of COVID-19. Instead, their faces appeared clearly on surveillance footage, and photos and videos of their faces appeared on social media. Yet no one was arrested on site. Instead, the FBI later asked the general tax-paying public to assist with its job in identifying these individuals once they had gone home.

White supremacy has already caused more harm in this country than any drug dealers could imagine. These folks have always spoken about breaking the law and then acted on it. These folks are openly noncompliant with the law, whether refusing to provide equal access to voting or to adhere to mask mandates during a global respiratory pandemic. But the Black drug dealers and the legions of imagined Black rapists and unchecked Black murderers have always taken precedence. Whenever this ideology, policy, gets challenged, lots of politicians give a fuck.

Major "Bunny" Colvin's experiment in Season 3 is a prime example of this. No one gave a proactive fuck about all the drug activity, cops trying to juke the murder-solve stats, politicians pushing their agenda, and people living in abject poverty until Colvin's experiment. Inspired by real-life Baltimore Mayor Kurt Schmoke's proposal to decriminalize drugs--effectively decentering them from law enforcement and addressing them as a public health problem--- back in 1988, Colvin is disturbed (as presumably Schmoke, who made a guest appearance on *The Wire*, was) with the amount of energy, time, and resources spent on going after addicts and low-level dealers with no fundamental change. From Colvin's vantage, these activities never led to improving life in Baltimore and left little energy, time, and resources for what he considers "real police work." Everything is business as usual. As the Joker said in *The Dark Knight*, "schemers trying to control their little worlds."

Attempting to effect real change, Colvin sets up three "drug-free zones," one of which is dubbed Hamsterdam, after the liberal drug policies in the city of Amsterdam. This is a unilateral decision, made without approval. It is amazing what someone close to retirement with a guaranteed pension will do. The sad and ironic part of this is that the experiment works, by reducing the felony rate 14 percent. A previously honest and transparent reporting of an increase of just 2 percent had inspired Colvin to try the experiment in the first place. Prior to taking this action, he is chewed out by Maryland State Police Superintendent William Rawls and Baltimore Police Commissioner Ervin Burrell for not juking the stats. No one seemed to care about anything other than the perception of "things getting better."

As Colvin takes steps to acknowledge reality for what it is and tries to contain it in one part of the city, however, everyone suddenly gives a fuck, despite his methods yielding the desired results. He legalizes drugs in defined parts of the city so that energy, time, and resources can be devoted elsewhere. There are five episodes in the show in which the drug-free zones are active, until Rawls and Burrell discover them and, predictably, lose their minds. But there is a short window when

Mayor Clarence Royce tries to spin this to his advantage, given the positive results.

When Black folks speak about accountability and the rule of law, there are too many proactive fucks given for anyone to keep count. No one gave a fuck about liberty and justice for all while so many are directly and indirectly denied both by our systems and institutions. But when someone starts talking about discrepancies and institutions falling short? Give a fuck, follow them, make them miserable, create barriers to basic and guaranteed human and civil rights, and execute them for everything from walking around in a hoodie to having an air freshener in their car. No one gives a fuck about the abject poverty, gun violence, racism, and disparities in the health-care system that led to COVID-19's affecting and killing Black Americans at disproportionate rates.

From 1956 to 1971, the FBI's Counterintelligence Program (COINTELPRO) was responsible for the disruption and destruction of Black folks speaking about this accountability. There were tremendous fucks given about this rhetoric, yet no fucks about the behavior illustrating the lack of accountability and the rule of law. Tremendous resources were spent going after individuals—everyone from Martin Luther King Jr. to Fred Hampton--talking about accountability. Today, folks such as Colin Kaepernick are ostracized for talking about accountability, and it seems like every day unarmed Black folks are gunned down by law enforcement while armed White folks in the same situations are kept alive long enough to be arrested or allowed to walk away.

There is always plenty of time, however, to proactively give a fuck about these issues, especially for law enforcement and politicians. It is always their turn to step up, as those who signed up to "protect and serve" and represent the interests and needs of their constituents without prompting. But, as we saw in *The Wire* and see in real life, there is a system in place that decides when it is their turn to give a fuck. As soon as folks start protesting about these issues, however, law enforcement and politicians want to give so many fucks that the message they should have given a fuck about in the first place often gets suppressed and lost.

In Minneapolis, there are folks serving longer jail time for protesting the murder of Daunte Wright than the officer Kim Potter, who pulled the trigger, did when she was arrested. After she was out on bail, there were more cops and barricades around her house than around the US Capitol on January 6, 2021. That right there tells you all you need to know.

We all suffer when politicians, law enforcement, security, and intelligence officials give a fuck when it is not their turn. History shows us this, and so does *The Wire*. If politicians, law enforcement, security, and intelligence officials were proactive no matter who the target was, everyone would be safer. It is time for these individuals to give a fuck and go after the disease and the folks spreading it and stop going after folks who suffer from symptoms and solely blaming them for their situation. With the system still intact, it is wise to listen to and heed Bunk's advice. Because two decades later and counting, it is sadly still the truth, making *The Wire* and its many revelations still relevant.

ॐ

ADOM M. COOPER is a Cleveland, Ohio, native currently residing in Washington, DC, who earned his bachelor's degree from the University of Michigan and a Juris Doctor from Syracuse University College of Law. He is a term member at the Council on Foreign Relations, a security fellow at the Truman National Security Project, and a member of the DC Bar.

The final shot of Omar and Michael K. Williams in *The Wire*. Photo courtesy of HBO

PART 4
The Incredible Lightness of Being
Omar and Michael K. Williams

Introductory Overview

By Ronda Racha Penrice

News of Michael K. Williams's death on Sunday, September 6, 2021, rocked fans of *The Wire* and other admirers. Most people were unaware of Williams's ongoing struggle with addiction. In a February interview earlier that year on *Tamron Hall*, promoting his film *Body Brokers*, about a recovering junkie who discovers how crooked rehab centers can be, he talked about how drugs and alcohol are not the problem but merely symptoms of the problem. He spoke candidly of not feeling worthy of the fame that came from playing Omar on *The Wire*. For him, folks calling him Omar was the beginning of him losing himself. Sadly, we now know how hard he was fighting just to be Michael K. Williams and be OK.

In his work, Michael K. specialized in allowing others to be seen. Prior to his portrayal of Omar, there had never been a character like him on TV. And if we're being honest, we haven't exactly seen anything close to Omar since unless Michael K. was playing another character. But the good news is that since Michael K.'s Omar, there have been more diversified Black male gay characters on television than ever before. Michael K. was a game-changer. Even when mainstream institutions like the Emmys, purporting to recognize all brilliance, ignore that over and over, time has a way of setting the record straight.

Scott Wilson's essay "The Power of Omar and Michael K. Williams" provides personal testimony of Michael K. Williams's impact as Omar. For him and so many others, Omar expanded their own humanity. Through him they saw a human being society had previously hidden. In part one of this volume, Ed Adams shared how real Omar was in his own life. So seeing him on *The Wire* was a recognition, an acknowledgment that had been a long time coming. And in tribute to Michael K., Wilson shows how vital Omar was in that regard.

In my piece "Reflections of Him: Conversations with Michael K. Williams," I share some of my limited conversations with him. While we didn't have very many of them, for me they were impactful, so I believe others might feel the same. Over the course of my two-decade-plus career, I have interviewed countless actors, but few have moved me the way Michael K. Williams did. Coming across a person whom I knew society had not tagged to make it but who did so anyway just made me root for him even more. Finding a way out of none is no easy feat. And when you go through the details of Michael K.'s life, there was a lot of nowhere to overcome.

I hope the tidbits of the conversations I share reveal a person, a work in progress, who did not just beat the odds but, through his characters, most notably Omar, revealed to others just how stacked those odds were and are against a lot of people. As hard as it is to accept Michael K.'s untimely death, there is comfort in knowing that his living was not in vain.

12

The Power of Omar and Michael K. Williams

By Scott Wilson

On *The Wire*, Michael K. Williams breathed rebellious life into what could have been just an empty archetype. He couldn't have realized then that Omar would not only become the closest thing the show had to a flagship character, but that he also would arguably eclipse the very show that introduced him to the world. Even before Williams's untimely death, GIFs and photos of Omar were used for memes on various social media platforms and message boards. But he meant a whole lot more than that to me, and still does. In my mind, he's an immortal window into a world that I was sheltered from during my upbringing.

Omar was born into the world as a supporting character on what I consider to be the single greatest television show of its kind ever made, if not the single greatest television show of all time. Period. To regard it as merely a genre show is to view it only in terms of its most sensational elements. It was not merely a "cop show" or a "crime show." Instead, it offered (and still offers) an unbelievably nuanced and complex portrait of how Baltimore's various institutions were affected and brought together by its heroin trade. These institutions were not nebulous, but part of an intricate whole. Out of that fact-based, fictional microcosm, Omar Little emerged.

An antihero for the ages, Omar Devon Little was the ultimate Robin Hood. He stole from the murderous hustlers who prospered from Baltimore's smack trade and redistributed that wealth among the common men and women who often became forgotten casualties of that trade's resulting block wars. That he always wore a duster was fitting, seeing as how he was clearly an early-to-late-aughts descendent (or update) of archetypal Wild West outlaws as they were portrayed in any number of westerns. When he strolls down the street whistling with shotgun in tow, one can almost hear any one of Ennio Morricone's iconic themes from Sergio Leone's immortal *Dollars Trilogy* playing on the soundtrack.

There was a twist, however. It came in "Old Cases," episode four, when Omar lovingly kissed Brandon on the forehead, making their relationship as lovers, not just partners in crime, crystal clear. To my heterosexual, cisgender eyes, that sight was far more shocking than that of Omar graphically shooting a dealer in the leg with his shotgun on the previous episode. My reaction was both swift and audible. I couldn't believe what I was seeing, and on an outwardly gritty show seemingly aimed at a largely male viewership no less.

Gay storylines were largely par for the course at HBO during the late 1990s and early aughts with shows like *Oz* and *Six Feet Under*. Still, this one felt far more immediate and egregious to me. In my mind, it raised a red flag, but not just for the obvious reasons. I didn't know it at the time, but Omar Little would go on to endear himself to me in a way that I wasn't at all prepared for.

When the Barksdale organization tortured and killed Brandon for not divulging information on Omar's whereabouts, I found myself feeling hurt and vengeful on Omar's behalf. When Omar identified his lover's body at the morgue, I was moved by the impenetrable mask of grief on Michael K. Williams's face as Omar. The great loss was apparent, and I felt it with an energy I usually reserved for the similarly aggrieved heroes and antiheroes of my favorite action flicks and revenge films. And, of course, those characters were all heterosexual, cisgender males. They were also mostly White American cops, soldiers, and vigilantes. Still, there I was wanting Omar to get his proverbial pound of flesh for the atrocity committed against him and his dead lover. That they brought it on themselves by robbing one of Barksdale's drug spots was wholly irrelevant to me. As Barksdale terrorized various Baltimore neighborhoods to maintain his grip on their drug traffic, Omar and his crew continued to terrorize and tax Barksdale for his ill-gotten gains. And I saw that as balancing the karmic books.

At the time, I imagined Brandon's murderers likely tortured and killed him as much for the perceived crime of being homosexual as for robbing their boss. The meeting Avon Barksdale had with his inner circle on the matter seemed to imply as much. I saw it as exceedingly cruel and sadistic. That's honestly why I didn't care much about Omar violating the street code of cooperating with the police to get back at the Barksdale organization. I imagine other *Wire* fans, part of the same demographic as I, likely felt the same way but, due to archaic notions of manhood, might be much slower to admit that to themselves. That's when I first realized Omar was becoming my favorite character and began to internally root for him.

Every time Omar came strolling over the horizon, or the show would shift its attention to whatever he was doing at a given moment, I found myself sitting forward as though I were about to stand at attention. He didn't even have to be pulling a robbery or engaging in any violence. Just his presence was enough. He possessed a coolness that breached whatever defenses my homophobia could muster. His duster coat and outlaw swagger tapped directly into the spaghetti western archetypes that my Jamaican movie-buff father had introduced to me at too early an age for me to really understand them. Omar was "Blondie" aka "The Man with No Name" for my generation and demo, but he was even better than that. He wasn't just an archetype, but a full-blown character. By the end of the first season, I was completely sold on him. He was my guy, and I was more than comfortable with that, his sexual orientation be damned. I grew to accept his homosexuality as simply a part of who he was, as much as my sexual orientation was simply part of who I am.

When Omar declared war on the Stanfield organization, I was

most definitely there for it. I loved the tension and suspense of the cat-and-mouse game between the two factions. I was thrilled to see how Omar became both a wraith and a trickster, exhibiting an almost superhuman ability to stay one step ahead of his prey while strategically dismantling them. Sometimes he would run and hide. Other times he'd bring the fight straight to them. Here was a man whom dope kingpins mocked for being in sexual/romantic relationships with other men, and yet they were not only deathly afraid of him, but helpless in the face of his constant onslaughts. I loved every moment of it, to the point that my enjoyment of the chase made me forget one of the show's many lessons: the Baltimore underworld it depicted did not operate according to the tropes of action movies and cop shows. Therefore, playing by the rules wouldn't necessarily have saved Omar, but repeatedly violating them was sure to put him in the line of fire one last time. So I was ready for Omar to come out on top, and for the dead-eyed sociopath Marlo to get his comeuppance by way of the business end of Omar's shotgun. Alas, it wasn't to be.

During *The Wire*'s final season, I was downloading new episodes a few days before they officially premiered on HBO via a message board. A few days before episode eight was uploaded to the site,

Time is running out for Omar in the final season of *The Wire*. Photo courtesy of HBO

someone posted a GIF of Omar taking a bullet to the head and dropping out of the frame, obviously dead. When I saw that GIF for the first time, my heart stopped and then sank. "NO," I thought to myself. "Not Omar! Not like that! NO!" Similar sentiments were being expressed on almost every related site and thread that I visited until that soul-crushing episode finally leaked. I probably watched the GIF a hundred times that first day alone, hoping it was a fake out on behalf of *The Wire*'s team to punish fans like me for undermining a show we claimed to love by watching a bootlegged version.

Watching episode eight "Clarifications" in Season 5 confirmed my very worst fears. I painfully watched as Kenard shot Omar dead in a bodega shortly after attempting to set a cat on fire. Though I knew the moment was coming, it still felt like a gut punch. I even winced and closed my eyes a millisecond before the gunshot exploded. This was no western. There would be no big showdown with Marlo's crew, no heroic standoff or hero's deaths. Instead, Omar was gunned down by a sociopathic child "just to get a rep," as Guru once rapped. It still hurts to think about it. But, looking back, I wouldn't have it any other way. Omar's unceremonious and random death fits in perfectly with the show's internal logic. David Simon and company did not half step or back down. They followed through, offering no mercy to my favorite character. And to make it sting even more with reality, Marlo never gets his just deserts.

A few years after *The Wire* debuted, I became a New York State correction officer. During my short tenure as a "prison guard," a term correction officers actually consider a slur against the profession, I came to realize men like Omar Little were hardly an anomaly in the real world. Contrary to popular belief, much of the sex that happens in prison between male inmates is consensual. More to the point, many of those men are some of the more feared and storied "street soldiers" among us. I've even witnessed some male inmates braiding each other's hair before going on supervised visits with their wives and girlfriends. Omar was very much a case of art imitating life to make the truth plain as day.

My stint as a correction officer exposed my personal prejudices as greatly unfounded. What I quickly learned is Omar's seemingly out-of-the-ordinary life marrying crime and loving the same sex was more routine than society acknowledged. Omar's human experience was no less valid than mine. I still miss Omar, just as we all miss Michael K. Williams.

In a world where the openly gay Lil Nas X has emerged as a rap star, garnering premier performance slots at awards shows, I can't help but think how Michael K. Williams as Omar helped make this possible. The years 2002 to 2008, when *The Wire* ran, were from a much different era than the one we live in now. Rappers were not allowed to cross the boundaries or challenge the social mores they do now. And neither were our TV gangsters. Yet it was during this stretch that both Michael K. Williams and Omar made their marks, leaving a huge impression on nerdy fanboys like me. Omar and *The Wire* could have arguably satisfied our collective appetite for street lore by providing something a lot less nuanced and challenging. Thankfully they didn't choose that route. Instead of serving us something off a fast-food value menu, they treated us to a full gourmet meal. Even as one of the chefs who helped prepare that gourmet meal is no longer with us, I am still feeding off its richness. And, for that, I am grateful to both Mr. Williams and Omar. May both their legacies (and legends) live forever.

&

SCOTT WILSON is a blogger, podcaster, and published author originally from The Bronx, New York, who spent most of his formative years in Lithonia, Georgia, in the Atlanta metro area. Wilson, who has over two years of experience as a New York State correctional officer, has written for such publications as *Don Diva Magazine* and *Hip-Hop Weekly*. He is the coauthor of the true-crime coffee-table book *Straight from the Hood: Amazing but True Gangster Tales* with noted true-crime author Ron Chepesiuk. His oeuvre as a blogger includes numerous articles for *Planet Ill* as well as his own personal blog, Scottscope.

13

Reflections of Him:

Conversations with Michael K. Williams

By Ronda Racha Penrice

I did not know Michael K. Williams, or Michael Kenneth Williams, as he would sometimes be credited. I did, however, have the good fortune of speaking with him three times—once in person, once over the phone, and once in a Zoom roundtable. Never for *The Wire* specifically, but of course *The Wire* came up. How could it not?

The only time I physically met Michael K. Williams was on the set of the film *SuperFly* in 2018 just outside of Atlanta. In that film, an update to the 1972 classic, he played Scatter, an OG mentor to Trevor Jackson's Youngblood Priest. He had a gentle spirit and humility that immediately gave me peace. He spoke quietly and intimately. On a set full of people, he and I seemed not to be reporter and subject, but either two friends catching up or two strangers becoming fast friends. As shy as he seemed, he made me feel like he wanted to be right there in that moment chatting with me.

We didn't talk about Omar in so many words, but yes, we talked about him in relation to life and Michael K.'s career. When he realized that he would pretty much play urban characters, he didn't balk. One of those reasons is that he was urban too. Did being "urban" mean he was not a person? And, by extension, his characters as well?

"No one wakes up in the morning and says, 'I'm going to become a jailbird.' You don't aspire to do that," he told me. "Those decisions are made out of desperation, and there's a series of bad choices and bad situations that makes a person believe that that's their only way out. I've seen it far too many times [happen] to good people, to good, strong-minded men and women who are intelligent, and they took their gift and just turned to the streets because that's all they saw or that's all they felt they had. And I wanted to shed that type of light to my characters when I played them, my hood characters."

At that time, he was experiencing a new milestone in his career. He was back on the small screen, on a Sundance TV series based on a book series of the same name playing Leonard Pine, a gay, Black Vietnam vet. "*Hap and Leonard* is my first starring role," he said. "That's one of the things I've never done in the past. I've never led a show before, and that comes equipped with a new set of responsibilities. I'm used to being the one that shows up and that rips it up. As Leonard on *Hap and Leonard*, I get to watch all these amazing actors come and do their thing, put their thing down, and I react to what they bring to the table. And it's a new experience for me as an actor and one that I enjoy."

When I asked him how he juggled all his roles, which were approaching one hundred at the time, and kept so calm, "family" was his answer. "I have my niece here with me. I keep good energy around me," he shared. "This business is crazy. It's a lot of energy, a lot of personalities to deal with. But if I got my family around me, I always know two things: I'm loved, and it's gone be alright."

The next year we spoke again. This time it was for *The Public*, a small film written and directed by Emilio Estevez about a standoff by homeless men seeking shelter from a bitterly cold night in a public library. In it, Michael K. played a homeless man named Jackson. When I asked about his preparation for the role, he told me that "there was no preparation for this. The only thing I had to do for this role was remember how to feel human, remember what I want to feel like. I want to feel love, I want to feel acknowledgment, I want to feel accepted. I want to know that I have food enough to eat, I want to know that I have clothes on my back, I want to know that I have someplace to live, someplace to sleep at night. You think these men don't want anything different? There was nothing to prepare for except to be a human being."

We spoke the day after rapper Nipsey Hussle was shot in front of the clothing store he opened in his Crenshaw neighborhood in Los Angeles to help jump-start and empower it. As a Brooklyn native, Michael was no stranger also to wanting to uplift his community. "The roles I have played, I am so grateful for them," he told me. "It has given me a platform to stand on to do the real work, like Nipsey was already doing. If I didn't have that, it would make it so much harder to get my community's attention, especially by young people, my little brothers and sisters.

"They saw me in my character, in my work, as someone that was telling the truth about what was going on in our community. So I got the respect, and what I do with it will make the difference. I hope to do some of the things that this young man Nipsey was doing in his community."

When I reminded him of some of his projects, particularly when he hosted "Raised in the System," the premiere of the sixth season of HBO's *Vice* newsmagazine series, where he helped expose the juvenile justice system, he responded, "I have taken my steps, baby steps, one at a time, because that's how things get done, one step at time. At least with me it does. And now I've educated myself, I've shared the information, and now it is time for me to do what I will do with the information that was given to me. And for me, it's going back to my community and getting into the heads of my young people, my brothers or sisters, my kids, and getting them to change their heads to start to dream, to start to hope."

During a Clubhouse session the night following the first reports of his passing, hosted by casting director Tracy "Twinkie" Byrd and other friends, urban streetwear pioneer Karl Kani noted how dedicated Michael K. was to his kids. Those kids from his nonprofit Making Kids Win hail from the same Brooklyn hood he did. Kani shared how

Michael made sure he talked with his kids. MKW's two programs, Future and City Arts Partnership, worked, respectively, to "reduce gun violence, the related deaths and incarceration of community youth" and to "engage youth in the arts and excel in school." So Michael K. was certainly getting his Hussle on.

In 2020, as the nation grappled with COVID, I had the good fortune to chat with him again, thanks to my membership in the African American Film Critics Association. During the pandemic, we had pivoted to virtual roundtables via Zoom, and he had the good fortune of playing Montrose in the bold HBO series *Lovecraft Country*. Set during Jim Crow, *Lovecraft Country* proved itself a unicorn and trailblazer for sci-fi and fantasy. One of the main points throughout the series is that racism is scarier than any monsters.

Unlike Omar, Montrose struggled with his sexuality, which I highlighted to him. While Omar never hid his homosexuality, Montrose felt he absolutely had to hide his. To pull the latter off, he said, "I guess I just related to the reality that I believe we all have something we feel uncomfortable about, or have insecurities about, or maybe have not fully come to terms with. I went there, in that universal space."

During that conversation, he shared how the Tulsa episode of *Lovecraft Country* made him aware of generational trauma. Perhaps that weighed heavy on his mind during the pandemic. Perhaps that trauma explains some of the nuances of his performance as Omar. "We all have trauma, whether it's from family members or from the upbringing or from the community or the circumstances in which we grew up in," he explained.

The genius of Michael K. Williams is that his performances hit on these points. Omar beckoned us to imagine other ways of "being hood." His very presence said that there was diversity in a place where mainstream pop culture had assured us there was none. If an Omar could exist in this ecosystem, who else did? So, while Michael Kenneth Williams is no longer with us, his legacy will live forever. And that, in itself, is more than a life well lived.

CONCLUSION

Why *The Wire* Still Matters

By Ronda Racha Penrice

Why *The Wire* still matters is a question some may ask every time they see the show randomly trending on Twitter, being discussed on Facebook, or attracting thousands of views for various clips. Podcasts like Jemele Hill and Van Lathan's *The Wire: Way Down in the Hole for The Ringer* treat the show as both a throwback and as something that has never been more relevant. In 2020, weeks into the pandemic, HBO shared that *The Wire* tripled its audience. This was almost twenty years after it premiered!

In October 2021, the BBC Culture Critics Poll crowned *The Wire* the greatest TV series of the twenty-first century. "*The Wire* has earned its place as the greatest show of the 21st Century," NPR TV critic Eric Deggans explained for BBC.com, "because there is no modern TV series that has better captured all the various ills hobbling the American experiment today, from ineffective politicians to toxic policing, vanishing labour [sic] markets, poverty-stricken neighbourhoods [sic] and systemic racism."

That heavy lift is a model that didn't begin to gain steam until the late 2010s and early 2020s, with such shows as FX's *Snowfall*, exploring the flood of crack cocaine in LA, from *Boyz n the Hood* screenwriter/director John Singleton; the Hulu hip-hop series *Wu-Tang: An American Saga*, about the early lives of the legendary group; and two shows from rapper-turned-actor-turned-TV mogul Curtis "50 Cent" Jackson, both on Starz: *Power Book III: Raising Kanan*, a prequel to his hit series *Power* exploring the early life of Kanan Stark, the villain whom 50 Cent himself had portrayed in the original series, and *BMF*, about the real-life Detroit-born drug cartel, from brothers Demetrius "Big Meech" and Terry "Southwest T" Flenory.

Unlike *The Wire*, these shows don't have the burden of needing sizable white audiences to be considered successful. Even more importantly, better metrics are available now. How TV viewership is measured has changed tremendously. Social media has made a huge impact. When *The Wire* first aired, Black audiences weren't being accurately counted. Also, there was no metric for social gatherings. So if ten or more people gathered to watch in a single Nielsen household, only the one household counted. Plus, Black families did not make up a huge percentage of Nielsen families anyway. As a result, Black viewers were not considered that significant. Then there is the issue of bootlegs of *The Wire* in Black communities. None of that audience was counted.

Of those who officially watched *The Wire* in real time, *Buzzfeed* reported back in 2014, 58 percent of the audience was Black. In today's niche climate, that percentage works. That, however, was not really the case in the early 2000s, when networks and cable channels still fervently courted White audiences while ignoring non-White ones. In the hood, *The Wire* may have been number one, but that distinction was worthless. With *Power*, which debuted in 2014, however, a non-White niche audience, especially thanks to social media and the expanding streaming universe, became acceptable in the industry or, at the very least, with Starz. Having that kind of latitude paved the way for other shows like *Snowfall* and *Power Book III: Raising Kanan* to have room to breathe. These changes, or evolution in the industry have had a positive impact on the development of Black shows, particularly in the vein of *The Wire*, by giving them more leeway and time to become great. Because predominantly Black dramas no longer have to rely on attracting a significant White audience, there is more freedom to cultivate content to tell their stories their way, giving them a greater chance to succeed or fail on their artistic merits.

The Wire, to be clear, is not a perfect show, which is addressed in the essays here. Truthfully, however, no show is. *The Wire's* enduring allure is not the result of it striving for perfection, but, rather, its willingness to get messy. Breaking out of the cookie-cutter cop-drama mold was a major move back when the show premiered. One of the most damaging features of the existing model was its general denial of the humanity of its Black characters. For a long time, Black characters were most often the criminals, while the officers and detectives were the heroes who cut down the bad *Black* guys. By today's standards, giving agency to the so-called criminals doesn't appear so radical. That, frankly, is because *The Wire* succeeded. In his essay "*The Wire* and the Games We Play," Odell Hall observed "crime dramas have typically denied this little bit of humanity to its Black characters." Being able to turn on a channel and see reflections of yourself or people you know is a privilege many White audiences have enjoyed since television's inception.

Oprah Winfrey, who was born in 1954 and got her first break as a talk show host in Baltimore, has shared that seeing Black or "Colored" people, the term of the times, on TV was so rare when she was growing up that it was a special occasion celebrated with other Black people whenever it happened. "We would call them to say, 'Colored people are on TV! Colored people are on!'" *Page Six* quoted Winfrey saying in 2015. It was also noted that Buckwheat, the notoriously stereotypical Black child character from *The Little Rascals* whom Eddie Murphy parodied on *Saturday Night Live*, was "the only black [sic] child she was ever likely to see telecast."

While seeing Black people on TV in the early 2000s was not unusual, those representations often lacked depth. For so long, comedy had been the premier vehicle for Black actors. Dramas with Black people in lead roles were extremely rare. And as was the case for most dramas, *The Wire's* writing staff was predominantly White and male. What was different, however, was that this writers' room had the benefit of leaders like David Simon, whose vision was sharpened by covering the predominantly Black Charm City for the *Baltimore Sun*, as well as Ed Burns, who was both a former cop and a former Baltimore public school teacher. Consequently, the show's Black storylines were more grounded and steeped in real life, real challenges, than those coming from other, similarly staffed writers rooms. Also, Simon, who carried

The Wire created many stars—maybe none bigger than Idris Elba.
Photo courtesy of HBO

the loudest bullhorn for the show, hadn't come up through the ranks of TV, so he was not indoctrinated into the industry's typical practices. So what might have swayed others in his position didn't even register with him. On top of that, he had a successful track record with the NBC series *Homicide: Life on the Street* and the HBO miniseries *The Corner*, both set in Baltimore.

Andre Royo, who played Bubbles on *The Wire*, admitted to me when we spoke back in 2015 that he hadn't recognized what *The Wire* was doing back then. Shaken by harsh criticism from some leading publications, Royo was rattled enough to actually speak with Simon about it in the middle of Season 2 and suggest he make some adjustments.

"'Yo, man, the *Daily News* gave us half a star. The *Post* said we were slow. Can we change it up? Can we do something different?'" he asked then.

"Absolutely not. This is the type of show that I'm going to do my way, the way I think it should be done," Simon responded. "This is the type of show that's going to be like novels that they will take off the shelf; when they want to rewatch it, they'll rewatch it."

Of course, twenty years and counting after the show bowed on June 2, 2002, we all know just how right Simon was. Without argument, one of the biggest difference makers remains its largely Black cast. In that BBC.com piece proclaiming *The Wire* "the greatest series of the 21st century," Deggans wrote, "By focusing its lens on the types of characters mainstream television rarely showcased, The Wire [sic] also gave us a vision of black [sic] people with the kind of depth US TV scarcely offered. The list was amazing, especially for that time: Andre Royo's insightful addict/police informant Reginald 'Bubbles' Cousins; Wood Harris's family-orientated, ruthless gangster Avon Barksdale; Idris Elba as Barksdale's lieutenant Stringer Bell, who dreamed of using business school tactics to build a legal empire; Sonja Sohn as gay police detective Kima Greggs; Wendell Pierce as McNulty's irascible partner William 'Bunk' Moreland; Felicia Pearson as a hitwoman character with her own name, Felicia 'Snoop' Pearson; and many more."

These portrayals moved the needle for Black actors, opening opportunities that few could have imagined at the time. Surely Idris Elba and Michael B. Jordan becoming major box office draws hardly seemed likely. And who would have thought these actors would be sought after for so many subsequent series? There were times when Black actors went years without working. But this is so not true for those in *The Wire*. As stated in the introduction to this volume, "Pick a show or film you like, and chances are someone from *The Wire* is in it." In some ways, they've collectively fared better than actors on shows like *Breaking Bad*, *Mad Men*, and even *The Sopranos*. Shows rarely have such high percentages of actors popping up in other series so regularly, especially a decade or two later. Given how large that pool is, it is quite remarkable.

The Wire also broke ground for Black characters. In his homage to Michael K. Williams in his essay "The Power of Omar and Michael K. Williams," Scott Wilson offered his personal testimony to the Brooklyn native's triumph in opening people's minds and hearts to a Black gay man. Ed Adams, in "The Otherlove of Omar Little," explored how that representation reflected family for him. In her "Walking *The Wire*" piece, Sheree Renée Thomas shared how close to home *The Corner*, the miniseries that birthed *The Wire*, as well as Royo's portrayal of struggling drug addict Bubbles, hit for her.

In that 2015 conversation, Royo shared how big a risk as actors it was for him and Michael K. to play Bubbles and Omar. "At that time, junkies for the African American community were so stereotypical that Blacks were mad that you played it and Whites [would] think that you're not acting at all . . . and homosexuals for Black characters was like 'OK, you're not going to work again.'

"That was a fear," he continued. "That's why me and Michael K. Williams, out of everybody on *The Wire*, kinda had this little bond, because we were both taking these risks with characters and hoping it would work out, and we [had] to trust our talent and trust that people were going to look past what they [thought]."

Looking back on *The Wire* now, in the aftermath of Freddie Gray's death in police custody in Baltimore and the advent of the Black Lives Matter movement, we can see that certain conversations about police brutality did not take place around the show. Mishandling and beating suspects and perpetrators was simply routine. So routine that not one officer truly challenges it. Instead, they *all* follow the script. Jonathan Masur and Richard H. McAdams address the omnipresence of police misconduct and the power wielded by the blue wall of silence in their 2019 essay "Police Violence in *The Wire*" for the *University of Chicago Legal Forum* journal.

Not even the good cops are exempt from this practice. This was established early on. When the cops raid the towers in the second season and Bodie punches Detective Patrick Mahon, the other cops unload on him. What's most surprising, however, is that Kima runs over to the action not to break it up, but to get her shots in. In that moment, Kima shows that her loyalty, right or wrong, rests completely with her fellow officers. It secures her spot in the brotherhood and dashes any hope of any decency being afforded to the Bodies of *The Wire* or the world.

Masur and McAdams point to the unwinnable war on drugs as the driving force behind such actions and assert that the problem of police brutality is addressed in the show as a no-win proposition. Considering that police brutality against Black people was a reality before the war on drugs, its continuation speaks to the anti-Blackness inherent in policing. That was certainly at play when Derek Chauvin killed George Floyd, even in the presence of an audience, in Minneapolis in 2020. In this respect, *The Wire* serves as a reminder, a record even, of just how prevalent police brutality has always been, even in modern-day policing. And one thing that Masur and McAdams correctly underscore is that it's not just a few bad apples, but instead the whole system that is rotten. Adom M. Cooper really drives this home in his essay "Bunk's Lessons About Giving a Fuck in *The Wire* and Real Life," especially as he ties in the Capitol riot of January 6, 2021.

When Barack Obama was president, he spoke with David Simon at the White House in March 2015. During that conversation, Obama shared that *The Wire* was his favorite show. Most importantly, he and Simon addressed the war on drugs, mass incarceration, and the need for criminal justice reform, noting the impact on the community at-large. Simon said that Donnie Andrews, the real person behind Omar, Obama's favorite character, spent seventeen years in prison and was prevented from helping to rectify what he had helped to destroy because he was a convicted felon, and that his story is one shared by tens of thousands of people, many of them nonviolent drug offenders. Obama and Simon also discussed the social costs of our many failures as a nation, especially in integrating felons into society, and how *The Wire* helped raise greater awareness of these challenges.

"But part of what your show depicted, though, is also that there's a generational element to this," Obama told Simon. "So you've got entire generations of men being locked up, which means entire generations of boys growing up either without a father, or if they see their dad, they're seeing them in prison."

And today, twenty years after *The Wire* premiered and over a decade after its fifth and final season aired, oversentencing, mass incarceration, recidivism, poverty, and other issues related to the criminal justice system are still pressing, which is why so many new people keep finding *The Wire* relevant. But it's not just mass incarceration and criminal justice reform that resonates. While the devil is always in the details, *The Wire* matters now because of its boldness in taking on the big picture by addressing the problems of urban America across a broad landscape. Baltimore may be the setting, but these problems, as addressed by Danian Darrell Jerry in "We Have to Save Us," play out in Memphis too, or any other hood USA. It's why Detroit native, mother, and brilliant writer Mekeisha Madden Toby can break down a specific incident in Season 4, the "education season," in her essay "*The Wire*'s Hard Truths About How Our Schools Fail Us All," and kick its questions out to the rest of us. And as Seve Chambers explains in looking at Season 5's focus in "Finding the Greater Truth: *The Wire* and Journalism," those failures don't apply just to Simon's former employer the *Baltimore Sun*. And the missteps I observe with the show's Black female characters not named Kima and Snoop in my "Girls in the Hood: Black Women and *The Wire*" essay are not theirs alone.

This broad stroke is one of the reasons why hearing from Michael A. Gonzales, Julia Chance, and Ericka Blount Danois in their essays "B-More or B-Less: Meditations on *The Wire* and Baltimore," "Reflections on *The Wire* and the Black Baltimore It Misses," and "Where da Hood At? The Heartbeat of Baltimore *The Wire* Didn't Detect" is so essential. At the end of the day, *The Wire* is one view, not the only view. Living in these communities and working in them make a critical difference that perhaps no TV show can truly capture. What *The Wire* does capture remains so essential that even twenty years later and counting, we still can't turn away.

Culturally, *The Wire* documents a time of pay phones and beepers. One of the most interesting aspects of rewatching *The Wire*, however, is its archive of early 2000s urban streetwear, which includes Jay-Z and Dame Dash's Rocawear, Russell "Def Jam" Simmons's Phat Farm, 50 Cent's G-Unit, Ruff Ryders from DMX and Eve's label, as well as the Black-founded Enyce, the Korean American-founded Southpole, and the White-founded Marc Ecko and Avirex, among others. Clothing is one of the ways in which *The Wire* established its urban authenticity. It also grounded the characters. For example, as Stringer Bell made moves to go legit, he began favoring button-down shirts and suits, while Avon, when he wasn't locked up and in prison attire, reflected his hungriness for the game by wearing bandanas, tees, and tracksuits despite being a kingpin. The understated style of both Avon and Marlo epitomized the "real gangsters moving in silence" ethos.

"For us, it's about giving them that hip-hop look that's also toned down and more subdued. When they are out on the street, they don't want to stand out," the show's costume designer, Alonzo Wilson, explained to Wilmington, North Carolina's *StarNews* in 2003. It also helped give *The Wire* a sort of universal appeal while allowing the actors to infuse their characters with enhanced personality. In other words, they made the clothes, the clothes did not make them.

My greatest hope is that *Cracking The Wire During Black Lives Matter* has given you new insight and reasons as to why TV is such a powerful medium. Representation doesn't just matter; it can change lives and maybe even hearts. It allows people to be seen so that change can be achieved or at least attempted, which is what makes me cling to the promise of Black Lives Matter. For me, *The Wire* scratched the surface, removing an important roadblock to showcasing Black humanity in its flawed fullness on the small screen.

Stringer, Avon, Wee-Bey, Bubbles, Omar, Kima, Snoop, Michael, Namond, Randy, Bodie, De'Londa, Wallace, D'Angelo, Brianna, Shardene, Keisha, Donette, Cutty, Poot, Marlo, Chris Partlow, Bunk, Lester Freamon, Carver, Marla, Bunny, Prop Joe, Butchie, Slim Charles, Dukie, Kimmy, Tosha, Dante, Gus, Clay Davis, Mayor Royce, Lieutenant Cedric Daniels, Grace, and so many others are more than just characters. Instead, they are a manifestation of the real people who form our communities, good and bad, especially when there are no cameras or newspapers to document our existence. And without them, there wouldn't be *The Wire*, and that's why it still matters to me, and perhaps to you too.

ABOUT THE EDITOR

Ronda Racha Penrice is the author of *African American History for Dummies* and its update, *Black American History for Dummies*. A working journalist for over twenty-five years with a specialty in cultural commentary and criticism, punctuated by an emphasis on Black history and culture, the Chicago native with deep Mississippi roots has held several editorial positions, most notably with the *Quarterly Black Review of Books*, and *Rap Pages*. In addition, she has contributed to many other publications, including *theGrio*, *The Root*, *Essence*, *Salon*, *Atlanta Journal-Constitution*, *Creative Loafing*, *Africana*, and *AOL Black Voices*, for which she also penned the weekly TV column "Remote Control." A Columbia University alum who also attended graduate programs at New York University and the Southern studies program at the University of Mississippi (Ole Miss), she also worked as a film publicist in Los Angeles, where she helped champion the very first *The Fast and the Furious* and *Bring It On*, among other films, before relocating to Atlanta, her longtime residence. Television remains a lifelong passion and love. Her work as a cultural critic, entertainment reporter, lifestyle journalist, and Black history enthusiast has appeared in numerous publications, including *theGrio*, *Essence*, *The Root*, *Upscale*, *Uptown*, *Medium*, *The Wrap*, and *Ebony*.

ACKNOWLEDGMENTS

When *The Wire* premiered in 2002, I and so many others immediately knew it was important. And twenty years later, it still is. Extra special thanks to Fayetteville Mafia Press for providing this platform to explore how *The Wire* fares in the Black Lives Matter era. David Bushman and Scott Ryan, I thank you both so much for your patience. Nothing has gone as planned, but somehow, here we are!

I still have to pinch myself that the incredible Art Sims designed the book cover! It's just that unreal. We are talking about the *man*, the artist responsible for so many classic film posters: *New Jack City*; Spike Lee's classic films *School Daze, Mo' Better Blues, Malcolm X, Do the Right Thing, Jungle Fever*, and *Clockers*; as well as *Love & Basketball, The Best Man, Ali*, and so many others. Thank you so much, Art!!

All my contributors are dope. Ed Adams, Seve Chambers, Julia Chance, Adom M. Cooper, Ericka Blount Danois, Michael A. Gonzales, Odell Hall, Danian Darrell Jerry, Sheree Renée Thomas, Mekeisha Madden Toby, and Scott Wilson, I thank you all for making one of my wildest dreams come true. Without all of you, there is just no book. I thank you all for taking a chance and sharing your thoughts and insights. I can truly say I have been enriched by your words. You all have made me see things in *The Wire* on a deeper level. You cover so much ground, and I am just grateful.

Sheree, you and I were once roommates in Harlem, and this is the first time we are sharing real estate together in book form. What a full-circle moment!!! You make up stories, wonderful and fantastical ones, and here you got super personal, helping me and I know many others see the real lives represented by *The Wire*, and *The Corner* before it. Drug addiction doesn't affect just one person, and the way you make that point hits me right in the heart.

Odell, you and I have swapped so many stories over the years, bouncing all kinds of ideas about how to express and represent the culture, and so it is so fitting that you are a part of this! Since the day I met you, you have always been supportive.

Ericka and Michael, well, Mike, I'm just trying to be formal, I have read your work for years. My bylines came much later than yours, of course, so to me, you both are trailblazers. Mike, you have been such an amazing cheerleader and actually encouraged me to approach Ericka! Without your encouragement, this would never have happened.

Ericka, thank you for being as cool as your writing always suggested you are. You could have said no so easily and for so many reasons so much bigger than any of us, but you didn't. And Julia Chance, wow, wow, years ago you posted a message in one of our Facebook groups that allowed me to explore Chicago house music in a way I never thought I could ever get published, and now we have explored something together that I could not have even imagined just two years ago! Thank you!! The three of you give Baltimore a voice, and that was so super important to me. So thank you guys again!

Ed, you are one of the hardest men to nail down for conversations these days, but I appreciate every chance we get to chat. Your observations always enlighten me, and here is no different. With all the balls you were juggling, you didn't drop this one, and that means a lot. And Seve, we have talked so much over the years I can't keep up. Without you, journalism would not have the spotlight it has here, and this conversation is such a necessary one. So thank you!

Mekeisha, you know how much I love reading your work. I can't say I know many people who love TV quite the same as you and I do. My Midwest sister (yay to the Chi and the D for joining forces for the greater good!), you have a way of breaking down the most complex situations in a way all can see! You do it here, and you do it in all your work. Thank you! Jocelyn (Allen) Coley brought us together on Nissan trips and I am so grateful to her. It is truly a pleasure knowing you!

Adom, Danian, and Scott, we don't have the history the other contributors and I have, but you all are tied to special people in my life who know me so well. Adom, Titus Olayemi Falodun, whom I have known forever, brought us together (thank you, Titus!), and he was so right. How you looked at *The Wire* and brought it up to January 6 is invaluable. Danian, you know how I feel about Sheree, and she was so spot on. The power of *The Wire* is that it resonates outside of just Baltimore, especially the conversation of how the poor, the Black poor, continue to get crushed in the process. It is so not just Baltimore. Scott, Allen Scott Gordon mentioned you a long, long time ago, but Odell is the one who brought you here, and I thank you for sharing your insights into your greatest show ever made. You speak to the power of how representation changes us all, not just the group being represented. And you came in in the ninth inning too!

To all the folks who have already written books about *The Wire*, especially Jonathan Abrams, author of *All the Pieces Matter: The Inside Story of The Wire*, I owe you much gratitude. You helped to frame so much for me. My friend A.R. Shaw also put me on to Jemele Hill and Van Lathan's Ringer podcast *The Wire: Way Down in the Hole*. I also have to acknowledge the streaming universe. Although I do own a box set of *The Wire* (that I have hidden for years in fear it could come up missing), I am super, super grateful to HBO and HBO Max for making *The Wire* so accessible. I don't even know how this essay book would have been possible without it. For me, going back to revisit what I read with the touch of a fingertip, rewinding and fast-forwarding, is just invaluable. I also love some of *The Wire* conversations that went down on Clubhouse. How incredibly timely!!

Of course, David Simon and, yes, Ed Burns, must be commended. Without them, there would be no platform. And then there is the cast, arguably the absolute greatest ever! I cannot name them all because it is more than just Wood Harris, Idris Elba, Wendell Pierce, Andre Royo, Sonja Sohn, Jamie Hector, Michael K. Williams, and the other more popular names. Everybody in *The Wire* helped make it go! Over the years, I have been super fortunate to interview so many of them. For me, as someone who covers TV, encountering somebody from *The Wire* is just another day! Yes, as Lester Freamon says, "all the pieces matter."

My friends and family are so numerous I just won't name them all because I don't want to forget anyone, but know I love and appreciate you all. I will say rest in peace to Michael K. Williams. To my mama, Tyrethis Beard Penrice, a forever heavenly thank you for all the things you gave me that I was too bullheaded to realize when we were together on earth. And, to my brothers, Raefeael Tylin Penrice and Darryl Russell Penrice, I love you both always! We've been through so much, especially growing up on the South Side of Chicago, which is one of the reasons *The Wire* hits so hard.

Now I also have to give a special shout-out to Wilson Morales, Napoleon Johnson Jr., Khalid Salaam, and, yes, A.R. Shaw and Odell Hall again because these are the folks who indulged my *Wire* conversations and just questions.

And to all of you who preordered this book or are picking it up and reading it now, thank you for caring and for showing that this crazy idea wasn't so crazy after all. God is so great, y'all, and I cannot even begin to share all the many blessings, including this book, he has bestowed on me.

ALSO AVAILABLE FROM FMP

ORDER AT FAYETTEVILLEMAFIAPRESS.COM

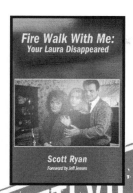
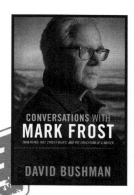

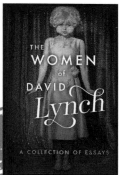

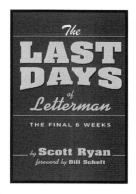